My
Staggerford
Journal

By Jon Hassler
Published by The Ballantine Publishing Group

Adult Novels
STAGGERFORD
SIMON'S NIGHT
THE LOVE HUNTER
A GREEN JOURNEY
GRAND OPENING
NORTH OF HOPE
DEAR JAMES
ROOKERY BLUES
THE DEAN'S LIST
MY STAGGERFORD JOURNAL

Young Adult Novels
FOUR MILES TO PINECONE
JEMMY

My
Staggerford
Journal

JON HASSLER

BALLANTINE BOOKS • NEW YORK

A Ballantine Book
Published by The Ballantine Publishing Group

Copyright © 1999 by Jon Hassler

www.randomhouse.com/BB/

Library of Congress Cataloging-in-Publication Data is
available from the publisher.

ISBN: 0-345-43288-6

Text design by Holly Johnson

Manufactured in the United States of America

First Edition: December 1999
10 9 8 7 6 5 4 3 2 1

For Dick Brook

My
Staggerford
Journal

Introduction

IN PREPARATION

I can trace my desire to be a writer back to the age of five when I was being read to by my parents and cousins and uncles and aunts. However, not until I was thirty-seven did I, upon waking one morning in September 1970, hear a voice in my head saying, Half your life is over, Hassler, you'd better get started. Obediently, therefore, after teaching my eight A.M. class that day—I was an English instructor at the community college in Brainerd, Minnesota—I went to the campus library with a pen and notebook and began to write "A Story Worth Hearing." Going back to it every day whenever I could find a spare moment, I gave myself two weeks to finish it, polish it, and type it, and then I moved on to my next story idea. By Easter, twenty-eight weeks later, I had written fourteen short stories. And now, twenty-eight years later, I have published eleven novels and I'm still writing every day.

Is "A Story Worth Hearing" a story worth hearing? Although I haven't looked at it in all these years, I doubt it. As a self-taught writer, I had an enormous amount to learn. Over the next five years, in the process of publishing my first six stories, I collected eighty-five rejection slips. On the hopeful side, I also collected letters from two agents in New York who'd seen the stories, liked them, and offered to represent me—if I ever produced a book-length work.

During these same five years I took up oil painting. My subjects were calculated to appeal to tourists—lakes, boats, pine trees, farmsteads—and I enjoyed some success selling them at summer art fairs in the lake country of northern Minnesota. But writing was my passion. I longed for time off from teaching in order to try my hand at the novel. Perhaps it was my income from painting, meager as it was, that gave me the audacious idea that I might be able to support my family over the course of a sabbatical year—audacious because the community-college system paid only half a salary to those on sabbatical, and no family man in the state of Minnesota had ever risked it. We were a family of five. My three children, Mike, Dave, and Liz, were students at the public high school in Brainerd, and my wife, Marie, worked at the hospital pharmacy down the street from our house. Sabbaticals were for the unmarried, warned my colleagues. What's more, scoffed my college president, St. Paul (the capital city, not the disciple) would never approve a sabbatical proposal for the mere purpose of writing a novel.

At this point Henry David Thoreau came to my aid. I remember quite clearly the afternoon we took up this passage from *Walden* in my survey course in American literature:

> *I learned this at least from my experiment; that if one advances confidently in the direction of his dreams, and endeavors to live the life he has imagined, he will meet with a success unexpected*

in the common hours. He will put some things behind him, will pass an invisible boundary; new, universal, and more liberal laws will begin to establish themselves around and within him; or the old laws be expanded and interpreted in his favor in a more liberal sense, and he will live with the license of a higher order of beings. In proportion as he simplifies his life, the laws of the universe will appear less complex, and solitude will not be solitude, nor poverty poverty, nor weakness weakness. If you have built castles in the air, your work need not be lost; that is where they should be. Now put the foundations under them.

These words took the fear out of me. From that day forward I ignored all warnings and submitted my proposal, which I padded slightly with academic goals such as earning a few college credits, developing a syllabus, and visiting several literary sites in New England. As soon as it was approved by the community-college board in St. Paul, I prepared for my year of freedom by converting my garage into my den.

That year of my sabbatical, 1975–76, is the subject of this book.

Before I began to write fiction, I had started keeping a journal. Early entries I made in a large, hardbound record book with pen and ink and a fairly legible hand, but soon I discovered that I was capable of a shade more vitality and wit when I wrote to friends—and one friend in particular—than when I addressed myself. Thus my journal gradually became typewritten carbon copies of letters to Dick Brook clipped into a loose-leaf notebook. I now have perhaps thirty such notebooks lying about my den, with at least 95 percent of the pages—and many of the entries in this book—addressed to Dick, a friend from my college years with whom I have enjoyed a steady forty-year correspondence.

As though to seek his blessing and that of my fore-bears in American literature, I began my sabbatical year with a trip to Dick and Charlotte Brook's house in New Hampshire, and from there drove out to see and photograph Hawthorne's houses and Emerson's grave in Concord, Massachusetts, and Walden Pond nearby. In Salem I visited the House of the Seven Gables and the customhouse where Hawthorne worked. Then, heading west, I stopped at Emily Dickinson's house in Amherst and Robert Frost's cabin near Ripton, Vermont, and then drove home as September turned chilly. I recall lounging around the house for a couple of weeks or more, idly reading and getting used to an unregimented life.

Then, casting about for a novel idea, I pulled from my files a fragment of fiction I'd begun a year or so earlier, a hopeless 174 pages about a high school English teacher named Miles, his burned-out friends, his bitter wife, and his dull job. It was a dark, unhappy beginning for Miles, because he was losing his voice and would soon lose his job. I was about to give up on it and put it back in the file drawer when I came, near the end, to a description of a typical day in the teacher's life: "First hour, Miles yawned." Nothing up to this point came alive the way these final six or eight pages did, and I figured out the reason. Nothing on the first pages corresponded in any way to the real world; everything had been wholly imagined. But now, here were the high school students I had taught ten years earlier in Park Rapids, Minnesota. I sensed how the rambunctious energy of Jeff Norquist, Beverly Bingham, Nadine Oppegaard, and Annie Bird (fictional names for real-life prototypes) fueled my writing, made it sparkle. Having appropriated these students, I guessed that by usurping their families, their entire town, its surrounding woods and lakes, as well as the nearby Indian reservation, I could breathe life into this book. Because it was late October in Brainerd when I began writing, I made it late October in Staggerford. The story begins, "First hour, Miles yawned." I wrote through the winter and finished in April. I have never since written a novel in so short a time.

IN PROGRESS

During the half year when Minnesota temperatures didn't drop below freezing, my nonwinterized cabin, seventy-five miles northwest of Brainerd, provided me with a private place to write. The property had originally belonged to my parents, who had built a bunkhouse for guests. This I turned into my study, and it was here, on the shore of Lake Belle Taine, that I actually began to write *Staggerford*.

However, it wasn't yet named *Staggerford* at that point. I called the town Willoughby (which proved to be too soft a name for the harsh things that were about to happen there), and my working title was "The Willoughby Uprising." It wasn't until very late in the writing that my subconscious served up the name *Staggerford*. I awoke with the word on my tongue before I was mentally aware of it.

During the first few days of writing, I entertained

large doubts about the worthiness of this project, but as soon as I introduced Miss Agatha McGee into the story, she convinced me of its worth. Spinster, schoolteacher, and conscience of the community, Miss McGee had been on my mind for three years, ever since I'd made her the subject of a short story entitled "The Undistinguished Poet," about a hippie writer who desecrates McGee's sixth-grade classroom with his toilet poems.

This tale grew out of an incident in my son Michael's school when he was in junior high. Michael came home one afternoon and proudly told me that his teacher had invited a professional writer into his classroom and that this man had read "a whole lot of poems."

I said something like "Wow, that's wonderful," happy to think that his teacher was reaching beyond the city limits for cultural excellence.

"Yeah, I guess," said Michael, apparently less impressed than I.

"What's his name?" I asked.

Michael didn't remember.

"What's his poetry like?"

"Sort of weird. He said 'shit' and 'screw' and stuff like that."

I was outraged. Open the classroom to culture and in rushed the barbarians. Who did this so-called poet think he was, scandalizing schoolchildren? After a day or two of my complaining about the poet's profanities, it dawned on me that I was behaving like some rigid old spinster, and at that point Agatha McGee stepped into my life and unburdened me. For when, during his reading, the poet makes the leap from his beloved toilet poems into the area of sexuality, and Miss McGee sounds the fire alarm and empties the school in forty-five seconds, I felt she was taking care of the issue of scandalous literature and I could move on to other things. Miss McGee subsequently entered several more stories and two more books (plus my current novel in progress) and fought countless other battles for me. Indeed, she took on bigger battles than mine. Last I heard, she'd brought peace to Northern Ireland.

All my novels contain at least one prewritten element like "The Undistinguished Poet"; some contain several. In *Staggerford* alone there are at least two others. Miles Pruitt's lengthy journal entry about his teenage crush on Carla Carpenter was originally an unpublished story entitled "The Cheerleader," and Miss McGee's first attempt at retirement was described in another story, also unpublished, called "Two Weddings."

And now we come, as every reader of *Staggerford* must, to the death of the protagonist. First I have to say that in the first draft of the novel, the reader knew from the start that this would be the last week in Miles Pruitt's life, for I attached a postfuneral episode to the end of each chapter. Then, second time through, I decided to try to reproduce the shock we feel at a loved one's sudden death, and I evidently succeeded, judging by the number of devastated readers I've heard from. My father was the first. I recall the night he came to the fateful page. He shot me a wounded look across the room and said, "Why did you kill my friend Miles?"

My answer then, as now, was that I was innocent. The Bonewoman killed Miles, and those who are unprepared for the murder haven't been paying attention. I received a letter the other day from a teacher asking me to verify thirty-odd examples of foreshadowing that her high school class found in the novel. Well, I don't know about thirty, but I do recall at least fifteen foreboding images, from the fairly obvious (Miles opening the back door and finding the Bonewoman peering in at him from out of the dark) to the subtle (Miles lying on a seat in the bleachers with his hands crossed corpselike on his chest). And why did she shoot Miles? Because she was driven over the edge by the rowdy, chicken-killing soldiers of the National Guard camped in her farmyard, which stood in turn for the overreaction of the government to a tempest in a teapot. In this regard, the novel is a parable. When I heard the final and awful news from Waco, I couldn't help thinking, Here we go again.

All of which does not explain, of course, why the author himself felt the need to knock off his protagonist. For this, I believe there are two answers. The most immediate reason was that I was haunted by a similar murder that occurred in the small northern Minnesota town of Clearbrook, near where I was teaching in the late 1950s. A choir and band teacher at Clearbrook High School, a young man of about my age, fell in love with one of his students, a girl named Shirley. In the spring, they married secretly, but because of her mother's deranged and intolerant nature, they continued to live apart. One night, taking her home from band practice, they were met at the door by her mother, who, having found out about their marriage, shot and wounded him. The teacher crawled to his car and drove off toward Bagley, the nearest town with a hospital, but the car was found in a ditch at dawn, for he had died on the way.

Why did this story haunt me for nearly a decade? I had never met this teacher, had never even heard of him before. Perhaps by developing a secret crush on at least one junior or senior girl during each of my early years of teaching, I found it easy to see myself in his place. Perhaps, too, as the years wore on and I wore out under the strain of teaching six classes a day and standing on hall duty between times, I began to see in this earnest, well-meaning young man the archetypal high school teacher sacrificing his life to bring enlightenment to these small and forgotten pockets of humanity hidden in the north woods.

IN RETROSPECT

One doesn't teach oneself to write in a complete vacuum. Although I credit myself with learning to write on my own—that is to say, without benefit of a teacher or mentor—I had, besides Dick Brook, a friend in those early years whose company was of great value to me. Jim Casper was a fellow teacher at Brainerd Community College, a man nine years younger than I, who set about to be a writer at the same time I did. We wrote furiously year after year and read practically every word to each other. We listened patiently to each other's failed efforts and cheered each other on whenever we turned out something good. It was Jim who coined the phrase, "the standup sentence"; that is, a sentence so cleverly made that the writer can't sit still with it, but must go to the phone and read it to someone, or, failing that, must at least pace around for a minute turning it over in his head.

My editor at Atheneum, Judy Kern, taught me how valuable an editor can be. Your editor has the objective eye you lack after looking at your work up close for so long. She dismissed my misgivings about Miles's death.

"What else are you going to do with him?" she said. "There's nothing ahead for him in life." She encouraged me to expand the postfuneral episodes. "This book is about the ongoing quality of life." She urged me to get rid of a couple of long, extraneous passages, one in particular being a dream sequence in which Miles meets Liz Taylor and Richard Burton in a bar and tries to stop a fight that breaks out between them. (It was actually a dream of my own; I had just seen *Who's Afraid of Virginia Woolf*.) I have since learned to use dreams sparingly in my fiction—they can be a serious interruption in the narrative—and always to summarize them rather than draw them out in detail.

Judy Kern was the sort of city woman who made me feel like a country bumpkin. Walking from her office to lunch one day, I watched from the curb as she made her way across a street in heavy traffic. Discovering that I wasn't at her side, she turned and shouted, "Come on, they won't hit you! It's too much paperwork!"

One time she phoned me in Brainerd to ask about some detail we'd already discussed. "I can't remember what you wanted here," she said. "I've had a stroke." Her stroke was a figure of speech, I learned after sending her my condolences on a get-well card.

"He will put some things behind him," says Thoreau, in the passage from *Walden* that changed my life. While I found it necessary to put a few nonessentials behind me in order to concentrate on the novel, such as reading the daily paper, watching television, and accepting social invitations, I had no idea that I was putting my family behind me as well. Marie, while continuing to work as a pharmacy technician, bought all the groceries during my sabbatical, bless her heart, but our marriage didn't survive many years beyond it. I did nothing to help it by closing myself up in the garage all evening during the school year and retreating alone to the cabin most of the summer.

At least three or four readers, including Hillary Rodham Clinton, have told me that they suspect *Staggerford* was my farewell to teaching. Which is true. Though scarcely conscious of it at the time of composition, I was putting the teacher in me to rest as I took up the profession of writing. Not that I didn't spend another twenty years in the classroom, but hardly ever again as a full-time teacher, and never without a divided mind, never without holding back a bit of my energy for my work in progress.

APRIL 1975

APRIL 6   8:00 A.M. The moon at three quarters stands icy-white over the peak of the house next door. Seven mallards travel east. The sun is out. The sky, despite what artists paint, is blue. Can a writer make it between 5:00 and 7:30 A.M.? Between 5:30 and 7:30 A.M., actually, for it took me a half hour this morning to wake up and shave.

APRIL 13   Up again at five yesterday. Showered and shaved, I was at my writing table by 5:30 and finished story Number 22 by 8:00 A.M. It's a zany tale called "Christopher, Moony and the Birds," beginning,

> *If I tell you that I, at fifty, am falling in love with birds, what will you think? . . . Birds sing-ing in trees. Birds on family outings, hopping and halting on the grass, cocking their eyes at the wormy earth. And of course birds in flight. What a consolation.*

Typed it and got to campus just in time for my 9:15 class of freshman composition. They write well and I told them so and gave them Bs and As. On my office door was a note from Tom Chesley, college counselor, thanking me for attempting a homecoming poem and assuring me he understood why I was unable to come up with one. Ever since I began writing verses for retirement parties, I seem to have become the poet laureate of Brainerd Community College. If he means he understands the fickle workings of the muse, I wish he would explain it to me. In poetry class I handed back test 1, awarded first prize to Betty Benson, and gave almost everybody a B or an A. During my office hour at 11:15, I reflected on how good it was to have finished a day's writing by 9:00 A.M.

APRIL 24   Yesterday the carpet was laid and what was my garage is now my den. I need this room more than my car does. It's a room 14 feet by 18 feet, and its one window gives me a view of my backyard with the bird feeder hanging from the lowest bough of the birch clump. Over here on this side of the room I have a stack of yellow paper and a typewriter and the journal which I started keeping in 1965 (I am halfway through volume 3) and fourteen notebooks I bought at a gas station for $1.54. And here, too, is the calendar I taped to the wall when I was working on a novel, "The Willoughby Uprising," in order to note the sequence of happenings. (I see that the novel began a year ago on September 6 and ended, alas, on November 5.) And then there's the dictionary, the thesaurus, and the pens. It's all over here on this side of the room.

On that side of the room behind me are a dozen brushes and two painting knives stuck in an old Folger's coffee jar. An easel. Three new canvases, 16 × 20, white and ready. My sketchbook, the third since I began sketching in 1965. Twenty-two oils, finished and framed, hanging on the wall ready for sale. I can calculate what each of these works will bring—$40 for the 16 × 20s and $16 for the miniatures. If I were a businessman, I wouldn't be wasting my time over here on this side of the room. I would move over there and work and work at trying to become a good painter. I would draft hazy landscapes instead of clear sentences. I am beginning to think there is not time in the day nor time in my life to do both. Thus the tension.

But I don't want to be a painter. I want to be a writer.

MAY 1975

MAY 16 In my recent stories I have been trying to inject more philosophizing, more editorial comment, more pointing out to the reader what he is supposed to think of the story. These days I don't believe you can say things between the lines. Hemingway and others of our heroes in college wrote between the lines. A professor would point to something Hemingway did not say and show us how Hemingway had said it after all, but not in words; he expressed it in the white space between lines 7 and 8 on page 49, and we would gasp and say, "Of course, there it is, plain as a pikestaff!" We called what Hemingway did good writing, and we called what we were doing good reading.

Why was I always so delighted to discover, on my own, a hidden symbol, a deeper level of meaning, a hidden theme? Was it the same kind of delight we used to take in passing pig Latin notes in grade school, in learning a password, in giving a high sign, in recognizing a fraternal handshake? Did my pleasure in Hemingway (and other reticent writers of understatement) grow out of a feeling that he and I were a secret society of two, and membership in this exclusive company was gained by reading between his lines? Whatever the reason, it delighted me then, and I am still delighted by that kind of subtle writing, and without realizing how unfashionable it has become, I have been writing exactly that kind of thing for the last few years. But the understated story is not the idiom of 1975. I have always been slow to see trends, and I first noticed the trend toward stories with a lot of platitudinizing a year or two ago. *Esquire*, *Redbook*, *The New Yorker*, *Atlantic*, *McCall's*—they were all printing stories in which the writer carefully guided the reader to the correct conclusions. But, I thought, let them go their way; I am writing a superior kind of story for a superior kind of reader. Well, I may have been writing superior stories, but I came to discover that I was the last of the superior readers.

"Why don't you tell us what happened to Smalleye?" asked a friend after reading a story of mine about an old Indian and a goose hunt. What happened to Smalleye was not important to the theme of the story in my opinion. What was important was what he attempted before he was injured and carried off in an ambulance. "Well, why don't you point that out to the reader, then, if that's the important point of the story?" Because I was brought up in an era when those things were not pointed out; they were there for readers to figure out on their own.

It seems today's reader hungers and thirsts for large direction signs in stories. They want to be told, "This, dear reader, is a truth about life." And it isn't such a bad thing. I am trying to write that way now, and while I enjoy it, I also find it difficult. I thought it would be easy, once I had the story told, to sprinkle a few generalities here and there. But I'm not good at it.

Yet.

MAY 17   Next Friday my creative writing class and I will have a picnic on the riverbank and read a piece from our journals. Then at twelve-thirty I will leave them (a spunky, interesting, earnest, good bunch of students) and I will attend a "party" for this year's retiree, a wise, gentle man of about sixty-two who is retiring because he has a cancerous lung and a cancerous liver. I fear it will be a wake service for a live corpse. Think of that class of nineteen-year-olds sitting on the riverbank in the sun, and think of the dying man, and think of me positioned exactly between them in age, without their youth and without his cancer, without their optimism and without his pessimism. There, on that day, the twenty-third of May, standing halfway between the young and the old, I will end my twentieth year of teaching. [The reader of *Staggerford* will recognize this from the retirement scene of Fred Vandergar. Like Miles Pruitt, I made a visit to this man's house on a dark winter afternoon, and everything was said and done just as in the novel—except that I, not having Miles's presence of mind, did not embrace him when I left.]

The novel and I will see eye to eye again when we're good and ready. After those 174 pages, coming back to the short story was like coming up for air. It felt so good, working on something so small I knew I could finish it in days instead of years. I turned out

one last week entitled "Some People Sneeze at the Sun."
I don't know whether it's worth a damn, but it was
exhilarating to create.

JULY 1975

JULY 13   For several years now, one of my favorite
daydreams has had me setting off on an afternoon walk
with Nathaniel Hawthorne, Ralph Waldo Emerson,
James T. Fields, Herman Melville, and six other friends.

This outing is for Hawthorne's benefit, but he doesn't
know it. Emerson has planned it as a way to get Hawthorne out. It is January 1863 and he has been moping
around the house for several weeks.

Reading about these writers of the first flowering
of American literature, I have always been struck by
the fondness they felt for each other and the prompt-
ness with which they came to each other's aid, and
this dream outing has always seemed to epitomize their
loyalty.

But not only was I born sixty years too late for this
outing, I was born thirteen hundred miles too far west. I
have decided, however, when I set off for Concord this
fall after twenty years of teaching American literature in
various Minnesota high schools and colleges, that if I
cannot join these men on their outing, I can at least see
where they lived.

JULY 14   Thank God I am not trapped in a store. I
am not a clerk, a manager, a bookkeeper, or a floor-
walker. Teaching affords me time off. When I teach, I
am free 180 days each year. When I don't work, as I am
not doing this year, I have, including both summers, 455
consecutive free days.

JULY 31   I am not, by and large, thought of as a cur-
mudgeon, Dick. I am basically the same nice, patient,
cooperative person you knew at St. John's. There are,
however, certain times during the year (maybe five or
six times) when the urge to be irascible takes me by surprise and with such force that I hardly think I can be responsible for what ensues. What ensues is probably not
all that terrible, usually a nasty, cynical, ironical remark
just funny enough to be forgivable; but it is evidence of
some fault or fissure deep in my psyche, and most
likely—nay, destined—to occur during the five or six
committee meetings I attend each year. Committees
(and that monster spawned by committees: the workshop) call up the worst in me. During workshops I am
not only uncooperative, I am downright unmanageable.

Late one afternoon, for example, half a dozen of
us gathered around a table to consider changes in the
English department curriculum. It seems our freshman
grammar course called "Grammar" was not attracting
many students. The German teacher and I were the first
to arrive, and we were followed shortly thereafter by
Midge from the cafeteria, bearing a plate of crusty
doughnuts. Setting them on the conference table, she
said, "Your chairman asked me to deliver these; they're
leftovers."

In came our nervous grammarian, in a turtleneck
and a hurry. Like Alice's rabbit, he glanced at his watch
and at the clock on the wall and said, "What are we
doing here?" He hurried to a chair and sat looking very
intently at the ceiling.

Then our department chairman materialized, with
the curriculum director. He placed the curriculum director in a chair at his right hand, and he himself sat in
the chair closest to the doughnuts. He offered one to

our grammarian, who ate it hurriedly, spilling sugar on the table. He gave one to the curriculum director, who ate more slowly, getting sugar in his mustache. Our chairman took one and set the plate down. As the German teacher and I took the last two, our chairman said, "That doesn't leave any for the president," and just then the president walked in.

"Would you like a doughnut?" our chairman asked him.

The president looked at the empty plate and then at our chairman, uncertain whether he was serious or joking. Our chairman was uncertain as well—no one as serious as our chairman should attempt facetiousness—and to cover his embarrassment he launched into an embarrassing explanation, which ended in an incoherent mumble.

The president, his large teeth outlined in gold, his blue suit rumpled, took a chair on my right and wrote notes as our chairman opened the meeting. While the rest of the committee opened their catalogues and prepared to fiddle with course numbers and course descriptions, I brought out of my briefcase 290 pages of student writing. "I have here the first six compositions from this semester's composition class," I said, my voice aquiver with excitement, "and on each of these pages you will see"—I spread a few dozen pages across the table—"a lot of red ink."

Everyone at the table sat stunned and open-mouthed. I had underestimated the power of 290 pages of student writing. Now, all of this red ink represents grammatical errors, I explained, and all of the errors were made by students who took Grammar last quarter. I turned suddenly self-conscious, too shy to raise my eyes to the faces of my colleagues, and the rest of what I said was delivered to the curriculum director's necktie, which was directly across from me and badly knotted. "I don't believe it does any good to teach grammar without teaching writing at the same time. Students have to see the practical good of learning all those rules."

Our grammarian was perched nervously on the edge of his chair. "Teaching the rules of grammar takes all quarter," he said. "We haven't time in that course for papers besides."

"But students don't need to know all those rules," said I. "They need to know only enough to avoid these mistakes."

Our grammarian grew quite agitated. "They have to know much more than I can ever teach them. At the end of every quarter I feel so miserable because I haven't given them enough grammar."

"I think we should go back to teaching freshman English the old way," I contended. "Include grammar, composition, and literature all in one course instead of separating them." This was a reasonable contention, but it was the last sensible thing I said. I am not a good debater and lose my grip on my argument, my words following my scattered mind off into airy quibbles and confusions. But my papers! Goodness, how eloquent. Those 290 pages were regarded uneasily for the rest of the afternoon, and every half hour or so the curriculum director nodded at them and said, "Maybe Hassler has a point."

"I wouldn't mind doing things the old way myself," said our chairman with uncharacteristic conviction.

"We can never go back," said our grammarian.

"We can never go back," echoed the German teacher.

"Let's change the name of the course," said our chairman.

This led to a series of nonsensical suggestions for a

name, including Language Essentials. This elicited a laugh from me and the curriculum director, a second or two before the president said he liked it. So did our chairman. But our grammarian preferred Grammar, thank God, and the motion was defeated, three to two.

Sensing that the meeting would end with our changing nothing, doing nothing, I gathered up my papers, excused myself, and rushed outside to fill my lungs with gulps of fresh air.

But twenty-four hours later I discovered in the local newspaper that something was accomplished after all. The name of the course changed, or at least its spelling changed, and teaching assignments were changed as well, for there in boldface at the top of our large quarterly advertisement in the daily newspaper were these words:

GRAMMER: Jon Hassler

AUGUST 1975

AUGUST 3 It's not a summer for writing. No summer I've known ever is. I have been mailing out a lot of manuscripts and getting just as many back. I may turn to nonfiction. I'm rather discouraged. I believe, as with Hawthorne, that my thoughts, like leaves, take on color only after the first frost. I've been reading Hawthorne's journals. In September I want to stand at his grave for a minute.

It was ten years ago this month that I began painting, Dick, and in those ten years I have learned, by trial and error, one principle: If a painter owns any tubes of green paint he must never open them. For ten years greens gave me trouble till I learned that trick. The longer I revise a story, the shorter it gets, and the more I work with color the fewer colors I work with. I may be working my way back to monochromes. Black and white. Or grays. Beautiful, beautiful grays.

Last Thursday I painted what I believe was my best picture ever—a few fence posts, a lot of weeds, a woods in the distance. It was 5 × 7 inches. Tiny. On Saturday I sold it for $16. And now I'm sorry. I wish I had it back. It was only the third picture I ever painted that I wanted to keep. But $16, I thought, why, $16 will buy me a night at the Thrifty Springs Motel on my trip east. Counting my miniatures, I have painted seventy pictures so far this year and sold them cheaply, because if I charged more I would sell less and I would paint less. It is my purpose to paint much. To paint incessantly. To paint six or eight paintings a week. Only when I paint at that rate do I perceive a slight improvement in my pictures.

In painting, unlike writing, I depend on absolutely no inspiration. I depend on a strange, relentless impulse that surges through me as soon as I open my eyes in the morning. Some days it's so strong I wonder if it might be fatal. Today I have not painted. Tomorrow I will paint six 5 × 7s. Saturday I will paint six more. That will give me a dozen. Then on Sunday I will choose the best of the dozen and try to do as well with a 16 × 20, but I won't succeed. My 16 × 20s are never as good as my miniatures. I'm like the would-be opera composer who discovers the limerick is his forte. Or the would-be banquet chef who excels at setting out the pepper shakers.

AUGUST 7   In the mail today, Dick, was a picture postcard from a former student saying my class left some kind of impression on him. Now, for a college teacher to have had an impression on a student is indeed a remarkable occurrence, and that is why I am remarking to you about it. When I last saw him, it was in the classroom and we were reading *Huckleberry Finn.*

The card comes from Hannibal, Missouri, and he reports that he ate at the drive-in where Mark Twain used to be a carhop, and where, if you are moderately hungry, an "Auntpollyburger" does the job. He says he saw the Tom Sawyer Savings and Loan office. There appears to be not a trace of authenticity in town. The postcard he sent, for example, is a *colored* reproduction of that famous photo of Twain standing outside his boyhood home in 1902. Early Kodachrome, I assume.

AUGUST 28 There may yet be a novel in the "Willoughby Uprising": third person.

AUGUST 29 Yesterday I went to campus and was asked so many times how it feels to go on leave that I came home and analyzed my feelings and found that I had none. I wasn't feeling any particular way about my sabbatical. I am afraid that after many years of steeling myself against various slings and arrows, I have become too stoical. By insulating my emotions against disappointment, I have insulated them against pleasure as well. Perhaps someday on my journey east the pleasure will break through. Perhaps stepping out of some motel some morning I will feel euphoric.

SEPTEMBER 1975

SEPTEMBER 24 "Success is counted sweetest/By those who ne'er succeed." Because Emily Dickinson (who wrote these lines) had a nice way with words, I thought I would drop in at her house as long as I was in the neighborhood. Her house is in Amherst.

I got to Amherst at noon. Tuesday noon. The streets were full of college students walking either to or from Amherst University, and I knocked at the door and was met by a girl in blue jeans much too young to be Emily, who would now be in her 140s, and this girl said, "Not yet." What she meant was that the tour of the house was not yet ready to start, though I had registered for the 3:00 tour and it was now 3:02. "You may look at the grounds." So I looked at the grounds: a long sloping lawn at the base of which is a flower garden, an enormous oak tree (the only tree left from Emily's time, the hurricane of 1938 having destroyed the rest), a two-story barn, a cedar hedge around the entire lot fifteen feet high and growing, a house next door hidden in an overgrown jungle of what looked like banana trees. It turned out that the girl in blue jeans was the daughter of the family that lives in Emily's house, and the house is not, after all, a museum but a private residence of a professor at Amherst University, and tours are restricted to two rooms: the sitting room and Emily's bedroom, which is upstairs. It was Emily's bedroom I was interested in, because the room served also as her writing room and her refuge against the world. The tour guide was another girl, not in blue jeans but in a jacket and skirt the color of tomato soup, and though I am by nature a fairly patient man, her commentary drove me up the wall, for she was not well grounded in her subject and she made up tall tales to entertain us. It is a corner bedroom, a high-ceilinged, airy room with two windows at the front and two windows at the side. It contains a huge oak bed with a bolster on the pillows and a divan and a chest of drawers and a manuscript or two in Emily's hand and, best of all, the table upon which she wrote. The table is nineteen inches square and faces one of the front windows. On the table is a small lamp, and on the windowsill is a geranium growing out of a pot. I wanted a picture of the table, the lamp, the geranium, the window, and the rainy clouds outside. As the girl continued her spiel, unsure of the facts and her grammar, I turned and aimed my camera at the table. I cocked the shutter, and began to squeeze the trigger. "No, stop!" shouted the girl. "No pictures are allowed!" The dozen tourists turned to me and scowled. I hung my head in humiliation. I tried to look as though I had not tried to take a picture and I didn't know where the camera hanging around my neck had come from. I waited for the girl to go on with her instruction, which she did, after glancing at me a few times to make sure I was going to behave myself.

Emily was always right. She was right about that picture I didn't take. I mean, before I went to Amherst I knew I wanted a picture of Emily's bedroom, but I didn't want the picture nearly as much as I want it now, having failed to get it. "Success is counted sweetest / By those who ne'er succeed." The tour, I'm happy to say, ended on a note of good fellowship when one of the women in the group fell down the front steps and we all picked her up and dusted her off and then the sun came out.

SEPTEMBER 30   I am home now, Dick. From your home in Ashland, New Hampshire, I drove my orange car to Contoocook; Concord, New Hampshire; Concord, Massachusetts; and then on to Lexington, Boston,

Salem, Amherst, Portsmouth, Portland, Quebec, St. Anne-de-Beaupre, Montreal, Ottawa, Sudbury, Sault St. Marie, Marquette, Duluth, and Brainerd. It was in the New Hampshire Concord that I listened to a campaign speech by one Don Dumont, who is running for president of the United States and has been doing so for decades, and whose proudest hour was one time long ago in some forgotten primary when he tied for fourth place in a field of five. He calls himself the "Happy New Londoner." He was reared in New London, Connecticut, and every four years, campaigning, he visits the other ten New Londons in the United States (including Minnesota's); this evidently makes him happy. The speech was delivered in front of the capitol and I was the only one there to hear it, although I suspect Mr. Dumont thought there were two in his audience, for I was standing next to the statue of Franklin Pierce and Mr. Dumont maintained eye contact with both the statue and myself throughout the speech. I had been taking a picture of Pierce when Mr. Dumont found me there, and he may have thought we were a couple of tourists. I was on the point of telling him that I was indeed a tourist, but Mr. Pierce was a native of the place and, if my memory serves, our only president from New Hampshire. But he gave me no time, being the fast talker that he is. Well, good luck to him. He may as well be president as anybody else, for all I care about politics anymore.

What I care about is people like Franklin Pierce. I was taking a picture of Pierce because I have always thought well of him, especially for what he did for Hawthorne. He did big things and little things for Hawthorne, for they were lifelong friends, and it's one of the little things that I like to think about most. Pierce turned up

Hawthorne's coat collar. Now there doesn't seem to be anything extraordinary about that, except that they were standing, at the time, over the open grave of Mrs. Pierce, who was being buried that day. Despite his poor health and a chill wind, Hawthorne insisted on attending the funeral, and afterward, at the cemetery, Pierce turned to Hawthorne, who was shivering, and turned up his collar for him.

Hawthorne later told this to James T. Fields, who in turn told it to me in *Yesterdays with Authors*, a book published in 1872.

The other Concord, in Massachusetts, has most certainly more literary history than any other town of its size in the nation. I had to pace myself and leave a lot undone. Not that I tire of hearing anecdotes about authors—I seem to have an insatiable appetite for human interest stories concerning writers—but I *do* tire of being taken through houses by guides who have memorized their speeches and gestures and who, like Don Dumont, have long ago quit paying attention to what they are saying.

OCTOBER 1975

OCTOBER 10   I went to Contoocook to see a covered bridge and because I have loved the name of that town ever since I first heard it spoken in act 1 of *Our Town*. I went to Salem to see the House of the Seven Gables and was allowed to climb up to the third floor by way of the secret stairway in the chimney. In Amherst I was allowed into Emily's bedroom, but she was gone. In Boston I spent most of my time in the Museum of Fine Arts, where they have seven Rembrandts and a fine bunch of Impressionists. On my way north I went through Gardiner, Maine, to see what they have done in honor of Edwin Arlington Robinson. They have done nothing, so I bought three doughnuts and moved on. For two days in Canada I moved among people who spoke nothing but French, until one night in a small motel in a grimy little town I met a man from Iowa who was driving his wife and his eighty-year-old mother-in-law to Nova Scotia. He was doing it in a most grudging manner. ("I'm damned if I'll buy new tires just for this trip. They say the roads in New Brunswick are terrible; we may not get past Quebec. I have to go now and help get the old lady bedded down.") All the while we were talking, the old lady was struggling to get out of the backseat of a two-door Dodge Dart and losing the struggle. The man's wife at this point, who looked like she was ready for anything, including a fight, said, "For years I've wanted to go to Nova Scotia, and he has dragged his feet! And now we're halfway there and he's still dragging his feet!" "Come on, Vera," he said. "We've got to get the old lady bedded down."

NOVEMBER 1975

NOVEMBER 3 Lo, Dick, I have been working on the novel again. Yes, this is the same damn story that died a most sudden death last year on page 174. After spending most of September and October painting the storm windows and trimming the hedge and raking leaves and doing what seemed like a hundred other chores that are at once onerous and diverting, I sat down for a day and meditated on the scheme of things and my place in it, and when I stood up I had figured out what was wrong with the novel: Pruitt was married. I went right to work. I corrected what it died of. I got rid of damn near everything it was saying about marriage (except funny things) and I got rid of Pruitt's wife, who in every chapter was putting in an uninvited appearance and casting a shroud over the otherwise wholesome happenings, and I installed in her place an old spinster named McGee I had had lying around in my brain for several years. I put her together with the hero, whose name is Pruitt, and they have set off together on what looks like a promising beginning.

I have been sailing along ever since, if not with great speed, at least with great sure-handedness and joy. I guess I have about a 65-page beginning, and there are another 65 pages from the last version that will lock into place at a later stage of the story, and I have a notion that those pages will represent about half of the finished work. The working title, subject to change, is "Pruitt and the Bonewoman."

But I have not yet seen the Bonewoman plain. Her face and shape are not yet clear in my mind. I have a vague idea that she is not as old as one might assume. She might have turned fifty, but not long ago. I think she has red hair and she wears it long. She never wears stockings, and I see red hair on her calves. That's all I have to go on at the moment. When I go uptown to mail this letter, I may have to linger on the street until she appears. I'm sure she's in Brainerd. (The landlady will turn up in church, I'm sure.) I haven't yet heard her voice either. You need more than one sentence from a person to get a good grasp of her voice, its timbre and tone. "Willoughby is a good source of bones" is all I've heard her say.

It's October in Willoughby and she rarely comes to the back door before dusk and maybe that's why her shape is dim. In alleys and backyards there are few lights. She turns in at the garbage can and scuffs through the pile of leaves that Pruitt raked together that morning and scuffs across the garden, where all but the cabbages have been harvested and the earth smells pungently tuberous, and she pounds with the butt of her fist on the oak door and sets off loud and hollow reverberations in the landlady's small, closed-in back porch. Pruitt and his landlady are having supper in the kitchen, and Pruitt goes to the door, so it is through his eyes that the reader first sees her. Perhaps she will be slow to speak. Pruitt will open the door and squint out at this shadowy figure standing on the bottom step, and say "Yes?" and the Bonewoman will reply with a question of her own: "Bones?"

NOVEMBER 4   To get these new ideas down on paper, I needed solitude, so last week I slunk off to the cabin near Park Rapids and turned on the oil burner and spent a week writing. It was a glorious week. I arose at six-thirty and thought until eight, by which time my thinking had made me hungry, so I fried bacon and eggs and ate sitting by the window, watching the thermometer struggle to rise above freezing and watching the morning wind ripple the lake. I was able to write then until about two. I go through a lot of contortions when I write. I jump up from the typewriter and stride around the table. I flit from window to window. I stand in the middle of the room and look at my shoes. During those six hours of writing, there seem to be two forces operating, one pulling me away from the typewriter and one pulling me back; thus I do a lot of pacing. And some writing. About 1,500 words a day. But by two I lose the struggle. I give in to the urge to walk farther away from the typewriter. The first day three miles, the third day five. I traverse the dirt roads of Hubbard Prairie. The sun is low and the breeze is invigorating and the withered grass rustles in the ditches. Then back to the cabin for fried potatoes and soup and a book to read and a glass of wine and darkness and sleep.

It has to rank as one of the best weeks of my life. For company I had a chipmunk under the house and a muskrat in the lake who kept sticking his head out of the water, either for fun or to see if the surface had frozen yet, and a number of squirrels. At seven forty-five and four each day a school bus went by, reminding me of the twenty years I spent teaching in the past and of the years I will spend teaching in the future. Reminding me how fortunate I am to have this year to myself.

But Friday it was very cold, and I knew if I waited much longer to turn off the water, we would have frozen pipes next spring, pipes with cracks in them, and so I put my typewriter in its case and turned off the pump and drained the water heater, the toilet, and the pump and let the water supply settle safely back under the earth, whence I would tease it up again next spring by priming the pump with a bucket of lake water.

NOVEMBER 5   What was it I thought of to write yesterday? It was a promising episode in the Pruitt novel. I've forgotten.

NOVEMBER 9   Now more about the Bonewoman. First of all, I don't believe that there has yet been in all of the world's literature a Bonewoman. I hope not. She stepped into this novel and I am most pleased to have her there because of her name and the mythic proportions she is likely to take on by the time the action comes to its melancholy conclusion. She is called the Bonewoman by the townspeople because she walks through the alleys in the evening and knocks on their back doors and asks if they have any bones she might feed her many dogs. You hardly ever see her that she isn't lugging a sackful of bones. (I am assuming that a sackful of bones, a gunnysack, would not be especially heavy.) She and her pretty daughter, whose name is Beverly, live in a gully five miles from town. The Bone-woman's sanity is variable; Beverly's sanity is intact, but she's crude. What drives the Bonewoman over the brink to commit foul and bloody murder is the arrival of an army truck and seven jeeps in her yard on a rainy Sunday afternoon. For the National Guard, it's a tactical maneuver, but to the Bonewoman it's kablooey. When the Guard leaves, the Bonewoman arms herself against whatever force might next intrude upon her property, and that evening, wouldn't you know it, Pruitt drives into the yard. This will be pretty close to the end of the book because he's going to get shot dead and he is the main character of the novel. He's the man who said to the Chippewa nation as they stood in the shade of the Ford garage across the street from the school, "Hello, what do you want?"

Later, after the football game, the Bonewoman shows up at the Stevenson house when Pruitt is there playing bridge with Mr. and Mrs. Stevenson and Imogene Kite, the librarian. Mrs. Stevenson gives her a beef bone, then back at the card table she claims to remember a time when there was, in this town, no Bonewoman. But Mr. Stevenson objects with surprising emotion and says that when he and Mrs. Stevenson moved to town, the Bonewoman was already there.

He says there never was a time when the Bonewoman wasn't prowling the alleys. Stevenson's problem is that he was told by a doctor that he has a bad heart, and in his subsequent passion for life he has fixed his attention on death, and for him there is in the Bonewoman a vague suggestion of the end of things. And since death is never far from the center of Stevenson's thinking, even (or perhaps especially) when he is at the office or the card table, he is startled whenever she appears.

Well, I don't know, I may be working with something too broadly mythic here, a symbol too obvious. I won't know until I get the novel pretty well in shape. In the gully where the Bonewoman lives on a tumbledown farm, Pruitt will die. For over a year I have known that Pruitt would die there in the dusk of an autumn evening, but it was only last Friday that I discovered it to be the Bonewoman's farm.

NOVEMBER 11 I once knew a woman who, when her husband died, started knitting. I don't mean she started after the funeral, when time hung heavy on her hands. I mean when she found him dead in bed she immediately picked up her needles and started knitting, pausing only to call the priest and the undertaker; and when they came, in their turn, she did not rise from her chair on the porch but looked up only to say, "He's in the bedroom," and tended, again, to her knitting. That was five or six years ago, and she has been knitting ever since. It cannot be called her hobby, because she knits the way we breathe, automatically, and we do not say that breathing is one of our interests in life. It *is* our life. As for her interests in life, she can turn her favorite chair to face her front window and watch people walk by, or she can turn it to the TV and watch the afternoon stories, on one of which last week there was a pregnant virgin and a recovery from cancer. She knits facing either direction. I have known all this for some time, but it is only now with time off that I have the leisure to bring it into focus. Her fictional name will be Lillian Kite.

NOVEMBER 20   New Hampshire is much on my mind, Dick. I have painted a picture of the covered bridge at Andover and another of the main street of Contoocook.

NOVEMBER 29   Listened to *Richard the Third* on the radio, following along in Mother's textbook from the university. Her notes in the margins in pencil and green ink, written fifty-three years ago—1922.

The Duchess of York says, "Accursed and unquiet wrangling days, how many of you have mine eyes beheld?" This could be Miss McGee looking back on her troubles.

DECEMBER 1975

DECEMBER 4   When I return to school next fall I would like to report to the faculty that I made use of my time. I would like to be able to say that I did the following things, and then list them in order of importance.

1. Wrote a novel of 380 pages
2. Painted 120 pictures
3. Toured the British Isles
4. Toured New England
5. Discovered walking trails along the Mississippi within two blocks of my house
6. Read 208 short stories

7. Read 30 novels
8. Took 3 naps

The teacher considering a sabbatical might consider the following:

1. Money: half pay
2. Unstructured day
3. Solitude

DECEMBER 9   Trying for ten pages a day on Pruitt. Passed page 100 yesterday—25,000 words. Yesterday Fred Vandergar's farewell party and Pruitt's meeting at the river with Beverly. I am unsure of the latter. The former is sound, but the latter is shaky. Today I should conclude that meeting and take Pruitt to the party at Wayne Workman's house.

At the party:

Wayne and Thanatopsis Workman
Ansel and Viola Stevenson
Coach and Stella Gibbon
Imogene Kite
Pruitt

Surprisingly few names, considering they represent the entire faculty in this book. And Imogene, come to think of it, isn't on the faculty.

Thanatopsis is pleased with most things in life, but not with her husband.

Wayne W. is pleased with very little. He is a complainer. He is ambitious. At the party, he will complain about the price paid for Fred Vandergar's retirement watch. He will be talking about Indian attendance.

Coach Gibbon will talk about sports.
Stella about the press box and her dentist.
Imogene? Knowledge.
Pruitt will ask about the Bonewoman's husband.
Costumes:

Imogene—cap and gown
Pruitt—park ranger
Coach—wrestling tights
Stella—cheerleader
Superintendent—farmer

DECEMBER 10   A pattern emerges now that I am
100 pages into the novel. After 8:00 A.M., by which time
breakfast is out of the way and the family is out of the
house, I spend a full hour and a half thinking, reading
over yesterday's installment, drinking coffee, imagining
dialogue; then by nine-thirty I am ready to type the first
of what I hope will be ten pages for the day—about
2,500 words. If I could put four such days together each
week I could finish by the end of January.

The party at the Workmans' apartment is off to a good
start. Wayne Workman is perhaps too morose. I think I
should make Coach Gibbon the morose one. Thanatopsis is perfect—happy and talkative. Imogene Kite is
dependably stupid. I think Stella Gibbon will be horny.
    I should be adding to my list of postshooting
episodes. Once Miles is gone, what will be reactions of:

Thanatopsis—?
Coach Gibbon—"I never understood him." "He
    thought a tie was as good as a win."

39

Beverly—devastated, cries with her chin. Structure
of her face seems changed.
Miss McGee—takes in Beverly.

DECEMBER 15 Nine pages today. Most of the
Workmans' guests have now arrived at the party and
I'm ready to show them in each other's company.

So far the men have remained in the kitchen and the
women in the living room. In the company of Stevenson,
Workman is obsequious, but Gibbon is not. Gibbon
keeps saying, "Aw, that goddamn Fremling." Tomorrow
Gibbon will fight with his wife. He will soothe himself
with his wrestling prospects. He will want to grapple
with Pruitt.

Pruitt will get drunk. He will taunt Gibbon by saying, "Who did you say you had at a hundred and sev-
enty pounds?" Parroting Imogene, he will call everyone
an "ack-comedian." And because she resembles Abra-
ham Lincoln, he will call her a "rail-splitter."

Imogene will maintain her dignity. She will tell Mrs.
Stevenson that a rail-splitter was what they called men
who split fence rails, not railroad rails.

Mrs. Stevenson will be grateful for this information
because she feels the need for knowledge. She and Imogene have the same ridiculous respect for facts, but
while Imogene is confident that she has a satisfactory
number of facts at her command, Mrs. Stevenson feels
underprivileged. She sits at Imogene's knee.

Pruitt should ask about the Bonewoman's husband.

Wayne will try to impress Stevenson with his Indian
attendance policy. "Befriend an Indian."

Stella Gibbon will get horny.

Stevenson on the subject of farming.

Thanatopsis leads a procession of trick-or-treaters.

Later she gets a phone call about the death of a friend's mother.

DECEMBER 27   It came upon a midnight clear. The flu, that is. I spent most of Christmas puking and shaking. Now I am hale again. 'Tis a wonder the way the human body restores itself.

I am at the crucial point in my novel where I have to write a convincing portrayal of a man and a girl in something like love—not love but something close to it because the girl is unreasonably dependent upon him.

DECEMBER 29   I am on page 142 of the novel. Yesterday I was on page 133. On the twenty-third of November I was on page 100. On October 20 I was on page one. I believe that tomorrow I will be on page 170. I have already written a twenty-two-page episode that will fit into the book after a five-page scene I must write next. That explains why 148 will presto! be 170. However, it doesn't explain the difficulty of describing the relationship between Beverly and Miles.

DECEMBER 30   The full impact of being on sabbatical didn't hit me until late October. I have been teaching twenty years, and during the first six weeks of this school year I thought I was still on summer vacation. So it wasn't until October 20 that I got down to work. Goodness knows what this work will amount to.

DECEMBER 31   By 1980 I hope to be living by my painting and writing, alone, at the cabin.

Looking back on that week in late October at the cabin, I see it as the happiest of my life.

JANUARY 1976

JANUARY 5 "The Willoughby Uprising" stands on page 199 and is moving forward. During Christmas week, surprisingly, I was able to get in two days of writing, and during New Year's week, three. I'm coming into parts I wrote in 1974, most of which can be used with little revisions; therefore, the pages are piling up faster. Saturday I worked on Monday and Pruitt's visit to Stevenson's office. Today I will put in his visit to Doc Dix's office. Next, a faculty meeting after school. Then Tuesday—his visit to Duluth, both the old folks' home and Karstenburg's office. This brings us to Wednesday. Shall the knifing take place on Wednesday?

JANUARY 10 Let me tell you what it's like to be on a sabbatical. When you're on a sabbatical, you're alone a lot. Your wife is working and your children are at school and your colleagues are working and the mayor is signing bicentennial proclamations and the dog-catcher is trying to catch dogs and the dogs are going around urinating on people's discarded Christmas trees and the butcher is cracking apart the joints of chickens and the parking lot attendant at the bank is clearing ice from the parking lot and the auto mechanic is replacing somebody's oil filter and while all that is going on—all this earnest and efficacious activity—you are sitting in your favorite chair surrounded by your books and your paper and your typewriter and your magazines and the figments of your imagination. You have been writing and painting and watching the birds at the bird feeder and before you know it another week has gone by and you realize suddenly that it has been five days since you have been uptown and seen anyone to talk to besides your family. Between Monday and Friday you have added thirty pages to your novel, bringing you up to page 229, and you say to yourself, before I write another word I am going uptown for a drink. You put on your heavy sweater and over that, your jacket, and your fur hat with the earflaps and your overshoes, mittens (a 1956 Christmas gift: good leather), and scarf, and you set out. It is snowing quite heavily and all the sounds and sights of the neighborhood are fuzzy at the edges. You walk three blocks before you meet anyone; it is a five-year-old pulling a four-year-old on a sled. But it is not really a sled; it is the piece of plastic on the end of a rope that passes these days for a sled, and the five-year-old is tired of pulling. He wants his friend to change places with him. The friend knows when he's well off and refuses. The five-year-old collapses then on his back and closes his eyes. Pretending to be shocked, you point to the boy lying in the snow and you say to his friend, "He's dead!" "No, he isn't," says the four-year-old. "He's just lyin' there." The five-year-old opens one eye and giggles. Well, it wasn't much of a conversation, but it's the best one you've had in five days, and you move on.

You find in the next block that you are catching up to a pair of teenage girls in the throes of a fit of silliness. They are pushing each other into snowbanks and laughing themselves weak. They both wear blue jackets and blue jeans and they both have auburn hair. The tall girl has straight hair and a good complexion, and the short girl has curly hair and heavy legs. The tall girl pushes the short girl into the snow, and as she does so, she drops the dollar bill that she has been clenching in her mitten. You point this out to her. "Look there, you lost some money," you say, pointing at the dollar nearly invisible already, under the heavy snowfall. The tall girl shrieks. The short girl shrieks. Dropping that dollar and having it pointed out by a man in a fur hat is the funniest thing that has ever happened to them. It makes you laugh to see them laugh. This meeting has a profound effect on you, because all week you have been leading an interior sort of life, and now, coming upon these two snow-covered, risible girls makes your heart leap. You walk with a light step, and soon the tall girl is running up behind you, trying to escape the retaliation of the short girl. It is an unequal race. The tall girl runs much faster. The short girl shouts from somewhere behind the curtains of snow, "Mister, would you please push her in a snowbank for me?" You would love to, but you are a man in a fur hat, and of course you don't.

In block six you meet Brenda Kessler. You remember Brenda from a class you taught last year. "How is it at the college this year?" you ask. "It's the same," she tells you, laughing. (What is there about snow that makes girls laugh?) "The bulletin boards have the same old notices and pictures on them," she says. "It's completely the same." "Then I'm not missing much, am I." "Not a thing. It will be the same when you go back. Except I won't be there." She laughs and says goodbye.

You find yourself now in front of the public library, and you go inside, shaking the snow off your fur hat and saying hi to the inscrutable, heavy, young, bored-looking librarian. The periodical rack is a disappointment. The *New York Times Book Review* is last week's and the *Atlantic* is last month's. You sit down with the *National Observer* and find one interesting article. It has to do with George Booth, an artist who draws those strange cartoons of dogs and bewildered people in *The New Yorker*. He started over again at the age of forty.

He got out of commercial art and began cartooning full-time. It took a while, but he caught on. I love reading that kind of article. I would like to start over again, this time as a novelist.

I move from the periodical rack to the new-book shelf, and there is *Humboldt's Gift* by Saul Bellow. I have read only one thing by Saul Bellow, a short story. It was very well written. I pick up *Humboldt's Gift* and read the first two paragraphs. They are very well written. I vow I will read *Humboldt's Gift*, but not now, for today it would be very wet by the time I got home.

I cross the Burlington Northern railroad tracks and enter the Log Cabin Bar and Lounge. I take a stool halfway down the long bar and Del the bartender serves me a brandy on ice before I ask him for it. I give him 75¢. Last year it was 65¢. I shake the snow off my fur hat and rest it on my knees. Here you look back over the last few months and you are amazed at the infrequency of your visits to this favorite bar of yours. You weren't in here once during October and November. It wasn't until Christmas, the jittery season of goodwill, that you began coming in here again. It was a matter of economics, your abstention from drinking in bars. It was a not particularly painful way to cut down on spending.

Two women come in and take the stools on your right. The one with the hair piled on top of her head has obviously just come from work, and she is full of complaints about her boss. "He has made that same mistake so often," she says to her companion, "that I am beginning to worry about his mental health. He did it Monday and he did it again today. That's twice in one week, and I have to tell him, but, God, I hate to tell him. When I tell him he gets super-pissed." Del says, "What will you have, ladies?" "A glass of beer," says the one with piled-up hair. "Me too," says her companion.

There is no one in the bar you know. You drink your brandy slowly and you watch Del work. After a while the ninety-nine-year-old man comes in and sits two or three stools down from you on your left. Over the years you have learned a few things about this man by listening to Del's remarks when he enters for his daily glass of beer. You know he lives in a small apartment above a store in this block, you know he will turn one hundred in February, and you know that the man who owns this bar (not Del) is planning to throw a sort of public birthday party for him when the day arrives. You know also that his name is George, both because Del always calls him George and because it seems that nearly everyone born in the nineteenth century was named George. Even some of the women.

Del asks you if you want another brandy, and you tell him no, you've got to get home. You stand and zip up your jacket and put on your fur hat. "Thanks a lot," says Del. "You bet," you tell him.

It's dark now and you walk home against the wind. The snow that made girls laugh has changed to a snow that stings your face. Rather than walk in the five inches of snow on the sidewalks, you walk where it's easier going in the wheel ruts in the street, standing aside now and then to let a car pass.

And that's it. That's the extent of your social life for this week. It isn't much, and you know it isn't much, but it's as much as you want right now, for you are more interested in what's going to happen on page 230 than you are in anything else. This is the kind of solitudinous life you asked for when you applied for a year off, and now you have it and you find it delicious.

But wouldn't it have been nice to have found, in that bar, a friend to talk to?

JANUARY 12   I spent Thursday reading what I have written—page 1 to page 299—of "The Willoughby Uprising," and I discover after three days' reflection and reading Flannery O'Connor and Cheever that what it lacks (besides completion) are two things: a flesh-and-blood Beverly Bingham and editorial commentary. So far the story is naked action and dialogue with hardly any explicit description of what people are thinking. A few paragraphs of the narrator's observations would give it ballast and slow it down a bit. One or two paragraphs in each section would do it:

> Pruitt's feelings about his father.
> Pruitt's feelings about faculty meetings.
> Pruitt's feelings about Stella and the dentist.
> Pruitt's feelings about Jeff Norquist and his kind.
> Pruitt's feelings about Wayne Workman.

I already have written his feelings about Superintendent Stevenson, the church, his four English classes. Thanatopsis. Needed: more of the same.

This comes so naturally in the Miss McGee sections. Why are they lacking in the Pruitt sections? Because Pruitt is me? Because I am habitually reluctant to express my feelings? Yes.

As for Beverly Bingham, it came to me as I was driving to see my parents in Staples yesterday that she must be talkative, nervous, crude. She must be this way each time we meet her.

The dentist and the doctor are a duplication. They shall become one—Dr. Oppegaard, D.D.S., and Nadine

Skethington shall become Nadine Oppegaard. This will also avoid the Skethington-Stevenson similarity in names.

Could Wayne Workman and Coach Gibbon become one? I guess not, yet they are both taking on the same irritable nature. I should make Coach more profane and dumber, and Wayne more fretful, more jittery, more whiny.

JANUARY 20 Story idea: The old friend who comes to visit and proves to have lost his vitality, wit, and intelligence—the things that originally made him a friend. He watches daytime TV.

Story idea: The man who wakes up in the morning with the premonition that this will be a day of momentous news. All day he is never far from a radio. He is braced for it. He tells his family and colleagues. The news, finally, is not momentous to the world, but to himself. Perhaps he dies.

FEBRUARY 1976

FEBRUARY 2 My novel finally has a title: *Staggerford*. Staggerford is the name of the town in which everything happens. It is the name of the town because one morning as I was getting out of bed and reaching for the light switch, the name came suddenly into my mind. The novel was already nearly complete (the first draft) and the town had been long incorporated under another name, Willoughby, but as I reached for the light switch the name Staggerford leaped from nowhere into my mind—nay, beyond my mind, it leaped onto my tongue. The word was on my lips as I switched on the light. "Of course," I said. The connotation of Staggerford (the second half of the compound as well as the first) is perfect for this story, and for small towns everywhere. It's perfect for my vision of life. Is not our life a fording of the river, a progress from here to the other side? And is it not a clumsy progress? Surely there is nothing sure-footed about it. The stones are mossy and slippery and the mud is sucky and the current is hazardous. Our progress to the other side is such a wavering dithering halting sidestepping falling-back strenuous somersaulting stooping stretching hysterical sorrowful giggly progress that from a distance it looks funny. It's a burlesque of progress. But burlesque of progress is, by God, progress; and Staggerford strikes me as a burlesque word. "Staggerford it shall be." That's what I said as I switched on the light.

Oh, the hours I have spent on this novel. I am not talking about all the waking hours of every day since October 20, when I began it (or the dreaming hours of several nights), none of which passed without my mulling over the story in my mind. I am talking about actual production hours when I sat here on this chair leaning over this desk and wrote. They were blissful hours. But happy as these hours have been, the largeness of their number tells me how much of my life I have poured into it. If it fails to find a publisher I will be all the more crushed. If it succeeds in finding a publisher, I will be all the more vain.

FEBRUARY 9   Read *Staggerford* to two of my colleague Joe Plut's classes last week, then had lunch with him and Ray Frisch, another English instructor, at Harold's Club, where we were joined by four of their students. Ray and I sat with Donnie Harrison, a pretty young student, between us and competed for her admiration. I won.

I also spilled my wine on my lap and told everyone that Joe is "wasting" his creativity in the classroom. I meant to say "channeling."

FEBRUARY 21   Well, I've got this sackful of fiction here, which is all of a piece. I've been working on it since the twentieth of October, and yesterday I finished it. "There," said I, "it's done and now I will set it aside to cool and in early March I will come back to it and begin revising it." But instead of setting it aside to cool, I got up this morning and began revising it. I couldn't leave it alone, not even for a day. There are ten chapters in all, and my revision stands at page 198, at the end of chapter 3, about a third of the whole.

I enjoy working on a second draft better than a first. If I had my choice I would write nothing but second (or later) drafts. But to get to that sometimes pedantic, sometimes exhilarating stage of perfection, polishing, filling in holes, rechanneling streams, etc., one has to struggle through the frightening first draft, create the damn thing through to the end, live it night and day and not know where it's going, or if you do know where it's going, then you don't know if you have the skill or stamina to get it there. It won't get there on its own.

The ending has begun to change. The sequence of events has gotten away from me. I must run to catch up. Characters are saying things I did not intend them to say. And doing things that surprise me. And I am being interrupted all the time by the life that goes on in this house I live in. I write a page and my son comes to tell me his car won't start. I write another page and my other son says he has a nosebleed. I write another page and my wife shows me her sore toe. I write another page and my daughter says she needs help with her income tax. Now these are all basically good people, and it is not their fault that their fuel pumps and noses leak, that their toes and tax forms need attention. I mean, that's life. If it isn't your toe, it's your tax form. And my novel is requiring all my attention. So I shall put my novel in a box and take it, along with my typewriter, to Blue Cloud Abbey in South Dakota. I will live with the Benedictines for a few blissful, uninterrupted days of writing. The monks make good companions. None of them bleed from the nose. Since they have no income, they have no income tax.

FEBRUARY 23   There won't be much discussion at the funeral of Miles Pruitt on Monday morning at ten o'clock, nor afterward at the cemetery because it will have begun to snow and everyone will be in a hurry to get back into their warm cars, so . . .

So the thing to do is to have the people of Staggerford search their souls on Sunday night, the night before the funeral, when they gather at the mortuary to convey condolences to Dale Pruitt (Miles's brother) and to Miss Agatha McGee.

Staggerford first learned that the Bonewoman was a killer when her daughter Beverly blurted it out in Miles Pruitt's English class. Her father had been put in prison for the murder of a stranger who came to the door selling kettles and silverware, but Beverly announced, in a rush of emotion, that her father had not done it. It was her mother. Beverly said this on Friday at about one-thirty in the afternoon. Twenty students heard her say it, and of course it didn't take them long to broadcast the news all over town after school was out. It would have seemed logical at that point to notify the Berrington County sheriff, who would then go out to the

Bonewoman's farm and pick her up and put her in jail. This move seemed so logically correct that everyone assumed it was being carried out.

But it wasn't. And the reason it wasn't being carried out was that the Governor's Giant said no. The Governor's Giant was a state trooper over seven feet tall who was sent out by the Governor to wherever trouble erupted around the state. Officially he was known as the Governor's arbitrator, not the Governor's Giant (which was Miles Pruitt's nickname for him), because he had been so successful at arbitrating differences between Indians and whites.

Those who are alarmed about the Bonewoman and who have tried to call the sheriff and his deputies have not been able to reach him. Every law enforcement person in the county (even the sheriff's wife, who serves as his dispatcher and cell-block housekeeper) is in conference with the Giant in the meeting room of the motel in Staggerford. The Giant is laying out for them his grand design for handling the Chippewas (only four Chippewas), and when Miles Pruitt finally gets into that motel room and says that the Bonewoman is badly in need of incarceration before something bad happens (he is particularly worried about Beverly), the Giant says absolutely no, no, no. The National Guard trucks at ten-minute intervals are even now driving down from Berrington and turning into the Bonewoman's driveway. The place is off-limits to absolutely everybody until tomorrow's meeting in Pike Park is history.

Miles is deeply disturbed to hear about the National Guard spending the night in the Bonewoman's (and Beverly's) yard. He wonders who is protecting the two women in that house from the National Guard. "The house is off-limits to the soldiers," says the Giant. "We told them they could sleep in the barn, but the house is off-limits." Miles suggests sending in one of their own troopers and bringing out the Bonewoman, but knows as soon as he says it that the Bonewoman could not be carried off without a struggle, risking the lives of the soldiers and the trooper, as well as Beverly, and he gives up and lets the Giant have his way.

On top of that, the murder of the stranger selling kettles took place eight years ago, and Beverly's father, wrongfully imprisoned, is dead. Certainly one more day isn't going to make that much difference.

So that's why the Bonewoman is free to make that great difference to Miles Pruitt.

MARCH 1976

MARCH 1   This afternoon I am taking this type-writer in to be cleaned and lubricated and to have its plugs and points checked. My capital Bs have become timid; my capital Ts, fainthearted. There are at least four pounds of eraser rubber gumming up the hinges, to say nothing of all the gray hairs I keep finding on the roller, on the keyboard, here and there all over my typing table. Every time I type I lose a hundred hairs. Every time I shower I lose a hundred more. Well, I can go without showers.

Yes, Dick, I am quite a good typist. Perhaps one of the best typists you'll ever meet. I was taught to type by a certain Mr. Brown when I was a senior in Plainview High School. Mr. Brown was from West Virginia. He had a large nose. He dressed like a fop and walked like a snob. He brought out both the best and the worst in me. For the first four marking periods I got As. The fifth marking period I got an F. The sixth period I got another

A. It was during the fifth period, sometime in late March, that I threw a typewriter out the window.

The question that interests me right now is this: could I have written the novel without a sabbatical? I am not sure of the answer. I will know more when I get back to the college and (in a year or two) try to write another novel. I know I could not have done it in the same length of time, for as I worked on it this winter I had time for practically nothing else. Without a sabbatical it probably would have been the work of two or three school years or two or three summers. Then I ask, has the sabbatical made as much a difference in the quality of the novel as it did in the time it took? I tend to believe that the sabbatical's bearing on the quality of the work was limited pretty much to the beginning of the work— those first two or three weeks in late October and early November when I needed hours on end to think things out, to see the plan in my head, to make several false starts and back up and start over again. After I saw the plan I probably could have maintained the quality of the work even if I had been teaching, but of course it would have taken me years instead of months. Could I not, therefore (when I get back to teaching), start a novel in the summer when I have an expanse of time and finish it during the school year, or in two school years? I'm not sure I could do that. The problem is that one can't start a novel when one wants to. Rather, one has to have the time when the novel is ready to start. It's just as likely to want to start on the first of February as on the first of June. You may be able to wait until the first of June, but the novel won't wait. The novel is more important than the writer. The novel will go away.

The value of the sabbatical is having the whole year open and ready for the novel should it desire to begin.

Where it stands: I am typing the third and final draft. The next page I type will be page 318. It's on twenty-pound erasable bond, and the first 317 pages, together with the box they're stacked in, weigh three pounds. I am able to type 25 pages a day, which means that in eight more days I will reach the end. I will wrap it up and send it via UPS to my agent in New York, Harriet Wasserman. That day I fear I will be the emptiest man in the Midwest.

For two weeks the snow has been melting in Minnesota, and nobody knows what to think. Most of us feel guilty, seeing the snow melting like that in February. It's supposed to be 30 below and we are supposed to be suffering. Maybe when Lent finally gets here we can be properly penitent. As for me, I can't wait for Lent.

MARCH 30 My family announced that we were going out to dinner for my birthday. I had been looking forward to a can of sardines and getting back to my typewriter, but I graciously submitted to their plans. Mike, Dave, Marie, and I ate at Harold's; Liz, who works in the kitchen as the chef's assistant, came to our table for a minute to complete the family circle.

APRIL 1976

APRIL 1 The novel is good. I am on page 375 of the final draft. To think I imagined typing this draft in four or five days. I have been typing it for nearly a month. I believe it's good because the narrator's wry, amused voice is consistent throughout. Also the story seems interesting. But most of all, the characters come alive. Such a strange, funny, suffering, exhilarating mix of people—like the population of every small town I've ever lived in.

Estimate of time spent on *Staggerford*:

October to January 30—	
15 weeks, 3 or 4 days a week	
6 hrs a day 55 × 6 =	330
February: 6 days a week 7 hrs 24 × 7	168
March: 6 days a week 7 hrs 24 × 7	168
April: 2 weeks 14 × 7	98
Total actual writing, not thinking, hours	764

APRIL 3 Completed *Staggerford*. This is the final copy—the third draft. At nine-fifteen this morning, I put page 475 in a box with the rest of the pages, and a great wind came up. Nature was shaken to the very roots of her teeth by the completion of my novel. My bird feeder swung crazily and spilled out all its sunflower seeds. The nameplate on the front door lost one of its screws. A large limb came crashing down from a neighbor's elm. It was an auspicious occasion. The most satisfying thing I've done since playing high school football. It called for a celebration. Accordingly, therefore, I got in my car and drove out to the Holiday Inn and ordered two eggs, toast, and hash brown potatoes. And I ate them.

Then I came home and fell asleep. When I woke up I put on my boots and went for a walk. Saw robins, redwings, wood ducks, and mallards. Came home and raked a tiny square of grass. Ate a tuna-fish sandwich.

As soon as the truckers' strike ends I will send *Staggerford* to Harriet Wasserman.

APRIL 5   The whipping sound of birds' wings in flight, like the snap of a rug being shaken.

The warmth of the sun on my back as I sit here in my backyard at the picnic table for the first time this year. It will be 55 degrees today—maybe 60 tomorrow. The snowbank in the shade of the hedge will not last overnight.

I wish I understood birdsong—not only what is said but who is speaking.

APRIL 8   To the cabin this noon. The fifth consecutive day of sun and warmth. It was 60 degrees outside and 40 degrees in the cabin. I threw open the doors and typed two pages of *Jemmy* (which I decided last night to turn into a novel). [This story of a mixed-blood Indian girl on a Minnesota reservation had several working titles; it would be published in 1980 under the title *Jemmy*. Although I wrote it as an adult novel, its editor at Atheneum, Margaret McElderry, decided to market it as a young adult novel because it's short and because the main character is seventeen. I am struck by how often this bright, promising girl from a deprived background turns up in my novels. Jemmy is Beverly Bingham reincarnated. I guess it's a result of having had so many of them as students in northern Minnesota.]

How is it that I am "up" for another novel immediately after finishing *Staggerford*? After five days' interval I hit upon *Jemmy* and could hardly wait to get to my typewriter this morning. It seems that if you believe in a piece of writing there are two lines of compulsion leading you forward. One is the strong, deep line that will sustain you until you either complete the work or lose faith in it. The other is the variable ability to write from day to day. It goes from strong to weak to strong. This morning I felt in tune with *Jemmy* and thought I could have gone on indefinitely. Then I picked up my paper and typewriter and drove to the cabin, thinking about the plot all the way. When I sat down to write at the cabin, I was empty. With the change in location my ability to write had gone from strong to weak. But I was not the least bit alarmed because the deeper, sustaining line of compulsion was still strong and I could come back to the story tomorrow and it would be just as good.

Losing the deep line, such as I did the first time on "Willoughby Uprising," is what I fear—yet losing it is probably a sign that the project is not worthy of my faith in it.

If only the deep line were not so hard to establish. I grope and grope for something to write about. All last year I groped.

How good now to have faith in *Jemmy*. Perhaps it is a period of heightened awareness because of the commencement address I'm preparing for late May and the tour of the British Isles I'm planning with Joe Plut for June.

APRIL 9   Again this year a dead rabbit in the well. Today I found him lying on his side, his blank eye open. When I threw him into the woods across the road, Ginger approached the body cautiously, sniffed once, then turned away as though with a shudder—as though she knew what death meant. Ginger, a long-nosed collie type of mongrel, used to be my parents' dog. On my way to the cabin I often stop by their house in Staples [a small town thirty miles west of Brainerd] and take her with me, for she loves the freedom of country living.

Just before I awoke this morning I dreamed that my former colleague Mark Bunsness was telling me how, just before he died, he had refused an injection of a painkilling drug. [Mark was the prototype for Fred Vandergar, the man dying of cancer in *Staggerford*.] He shook his head at the nurse. "Penance" was the only word he could utter, and the nurse did not understand. "Penance," he said again, and he folded his hands to indicate that the reason was religious. The nurse understood and was angered. She slammed the syringe down on the hospital tray and stormed out of the room.

Mark was telling me this in my dream in his best storytelling manner, imitating himself folding his hands and imitating the nurse in her anger.

It did not strike me as odd that he should be telling me this after his death. A dead man speaking didn't seem strange until I began to write it down. Writing brings out the true aspect of things . . . the oddness of things, which should be obvious.

It took me twenty-four hours to get the cabin pump working, my rake broke, a birch tree came down in the wind, writing was hard work. Some days daily life is uphill.

APRIL 10   At the state convention of the Minnesota Council of Teachers of English in Willmar, which I approached with little enthusiasm and a head full of snot, my New England slide presentation, which I had put together from my trip to New England, was the highlight of the small group sessions. "Where can I buy it?" asked a teacher. Even Ray Milowski—a Hawthorne expert—said it was good. (My voice shook as I spoke to the group. Why, at forty-three, am I still so meek?)

I had thought that by agreeing to be commencement speaker I would keep my mind alive after finishing *Staggerford*. But instead, it has caused me to worry and keeps me from my fiction. If I could write the speech and forget it, I could turn to other things, but I can't think of what to write. I have very little in the way of advice to hand down to graduates.

The one-page letter I wrote to Dick Brook yesterday was so uninspired that I dug a pretty good ink drawing out of the wastebasket and enclosed it with the letter.

APRIL 11 I have no classes today. This is the 150th consecutive school day on which I have had no classes. It sounds like the beginning of a novel. "He had not had a class for 150 days, and he was called unlucky."

The flight to Ireland Joe Plut and I had intended to take was canceled for lack of takers. A month ago, Joe talked me into taking this trip, and I am apprehensive. I have never been on a plane, much less overseas. I am now scheduled to leave on June 9 and return on July 1—a three-week trip instead of the four-week trip I had originally planned. But that's okay because it will be summer and I will be anxious to get back to the cabin.

APRIL 12 Winter came late and left early. The last trace of snow will disappear from my yard today. Last year it disappeared one month later—the seventh of

May. The sun has been out since last Thursday. Except at night. My yard is raked. Robins are flying loop-the-loops in the sky. I have already seen mourning doves, blackbirds, wood ducks, hawks, and geese. "How was your winter in the South?" I ask them all. "Fine," they say, "it's always fine. The weather is comfortable and the accommodations were satisfactory, but how we love to come back to Minnesota."

"And how I love to see you back," I call after them, but they do not hear me. They are already out of earshot, looping the loop over the river north of town.

APRIL 14   Flies. I ventured up to the cabin yesterday and stayed overnight—earlier in the year than ever before. I lit the oil burner, and as the cabin began to heat up, a number of flies came staggering, Lazarus-like, out of the window casings. One of them flew a short ways, then stopped to do whatever flies do instead of yawn. He seemed to be scratching his belly, trying to recall, I suppose, the interesting dream he had just awakened from. All evening these flies sat around the living room looking dismal. Occasionally one would attempt a liftoff and bump his head on the wall. The following day they were still groggy—one of them landing splay-legged beside some sugar I spilled and turning his back on it. Next week when I return I will kill them all.

I set off from the cabin in mid-afternoon, walking west down the tar road, and I met my neighbor Mrs. L., who was wavering slowly toward me on her bike. Last year she could recognize me from farther away, but that was before her diabetes began draining the sight from her eyes, and now she answered my wave and my greeting and was practically on top of me before she knew who she was talking to. She told me that last week in her apartment in Minneapolis she chased a man out of her living room. He left by the window because that was the way he came in. She invited me to supper. I accepted, for my cupboard holds only such things as a small can of ground sage and an old envelope of Kool-Aid.

A bit farther down the tar road I met her husband, Mr. L., weaving slowly toward me in his car, to the right side of which was tied an eight-foot board, number-one-grade knotless pine, which will become part of the garage he is building with his own two hands. He invited me to supper. I accepted, for my cupboard holds only such things as a package of tasteless cones for ice cream and a box of dusty toothpicks.

A bit farther down the road I came to the end. I turned south on a road that led past a farmhouse on the right and a farmhouse on the left, through a marsh at the bottom of the hill, then up again to a farm at the top of the next hill. This distance (one mile) I covered with Ginger running back and forth beside me in the ditch. She was ecstatic; she was off the leash for the first time all winter; she splashed into a muddy creek and came out trailing a thorny stem behind her. She leapt through a barbed-wire fence (losing the stem) in order to chase a blackbird off a dry cowpie. The only way she could convey to me her limitless happiness was to rush at me and bite me hard on the boot.

I was not wearing much for April, but April this year (bless it) has decided to be May, and I was hot. I unzipped my jacket and carried it. My dog thought this wise of me and she bit me on the boot again.

I assumed it was between four and five o'clock (I seldom wind my watch), but when I reached the vicinity of the cabin Mr. L. was out on his bike looking for me. I had lost track of time.

Supper was ready. It was past ready. It was six.

But the sun was still up and warm. I was confused, like the flies coming out of the window casing; I was emerging from winter vaguely bewildered.

MAY 1976

MAY 9   The commencement address has been weighing heavily on my mind. I mull over what I shall say and how I shall keep my voice from shaking, the sort of obsession with one's public image that one should have outgrown when one was eighteen.

So *Jemmy* rests on page 50 with Jemmy lost in a blizzard and taking refuge in a barn, warming herself in the stall of a shaggy horse who goes by the name of Old Socky.

MAY 10   What about the solitude of the four New England writers whose homes I visited?

Frost's cabin on a mountaintop, Emily's upstairs bedroom, Hawthorne's tower at the Wayside, Thoreau's cabin in the woods. Their most obvious common trait was their desire to be alone. They had interior lives to lead. Their wisdom grew out of self-sufficiency.

The wisdom handed down by these four writers grew out of periods of reflection as well as periods of social commerce. They sought a balance between society and solitude.

We are not all alike in our need to be alone. Very few of us have the appetite for solitude that Emily Dickinson had; she did not leave her house for months at a time. Even Thoreau, who is thought of by some as a hermit, came out of the woods every day or two in order to visit with his friends in Concord. (Isn't it ironic that a town named Concord should be the first battleground of the Revolutionary War?) He said that the gossip he heard there was as refreshing as the rustling of leaves—implying, perhaps, that it was also as meaningful.

MAY 30 My commencement address, a rather pointless account of my trip to New England, came off without a hitch or mishap. Everyone applauded politely and then retired to the college cafeteria for punch and nuts.

JUNE 1976

JUNE 2 To the cabin with son David. Up at seven-fifteen with the sun shining in the cabin bedroom and the birds singing loudly. Out to the bunkhouse to continue writing chapter 16 of *Four Miles to Pinecone*, which Margaret Lichtenberg is waiting for at Frederick Warne.

David is up at nine, early for him, and we eat toast and shredded wheat. By noon I am finished with chapter 16 and David is reading chapter 5. We go down to the lake and finish building the dock—an ugly, sturdy structure. The last one I intend to build. After this we will buy ready-made sections and put them in with pipe.

JULY 1976

JULY 8 Arrived home from the British Isles one week ago. Have wanted to talk about my trip ever since—have said more than even my parents care to hear.

JULY 11 Through Great Britain with Joe Plut, a veteran traveler. Joe does not care for life as much as he cares for representations of life. "The play's the thing." He ignores the drama of the city of London as he rushes headlong to the theater. Touring Ireland, he has eyes only for the sights listed in guidebooks.

I lost my heart a number of times in the British Isles. (I am talking about an unpremeditated quickening of the heartbeat, an unexpected surge of joy.) Number one was my first morning in London, when I discovered that the fabled landmarks of that city were not only real and tangible but within walking distance of our hotel. Teaching English literature for twenty years, one tends to think of such things as Westminster Abbey and the Tower and St. Paul's as the products of poetic imagination, like Camelot. Walking into them finally was like stepping into a myth. (On my first visit to Westminster I wasn't allowed in because the Queen was inside. Did they think I would disturb her prayers?)

Number two was at the curtain call of *The Winter's Tale* in Stratford-upon-Avon. It was a greatly moving performance of a play I had been unfamiliar with, and as it ended I was exhilarated by the thought of watching Shakespeare in the town where he was born and reared and where he died and was buried and where for 350 years, pilgrims (beginning with Ben Jonson) have been coming to pay their respects to his vast imagination. Another good memory from Stratford concerns Joe Plut, who tries to act very English. On the way over he gave me a number of hints on how to avoid seeming like what I was, an American. One hint was that in ordering bacon for breakfast I should not ask for bacon. I should say *rashers*, as the English do. It was in Stratford that Joe asked for rashers and the waiter said, "You mean bacon?"

Number three was in the rolling Cotswolds of central England. We were on a bus traveling from Stratford to Oxford and I couldn't keep my eyes off the valleys and hills and hedgerows and a number of hamlets with quaint names like Chipping Norton where, because it was Sunday morning, bells were ringing in old stone churches.

Number four was in the Wicklow Mountains as we climbed out of Dublin in our rented car. This was my first look at Ireland's green beauty that everyone talks about but which has to be seen firsthand to be understood. It differs from the Cotswolds in that it is more rugged and the vistas are broader and the farms are smaller and the sheep have a brogue.

Number five was in the farmhouse of Patrick Meany and his family, my Kilkenny cousins. I called their farm from the town of Kilkenny. Their son, John, used to correspond with my son Mike when they were both junior-high age, and when I reminded Mrs. Meany of this and said I was Mike's father, she got very interested and invited Joe and me out at 9:00 P.M., when chores were done. The first thing they did when we arrived was to take us for a lovely ride to a distant hilltop where they were pasturing some of their cattle and where we could see the Wicklow Mountains through which we had come and also the peaks of hills on the south coast. Then back at their house we drank large glassfuls of Hennessy cognac and visited until eleven-thirty, when at a signal from Mrs. Meany, the older children served tea, which consisted of (besides tea) ham sandwiches, cake, pie, and cookies. Patrick spoke of his grandmother, who was born in the 1840s and lived to be ninety-two and told him stories of the potato famine. John, the eldest son, attends Cork University and intends to become a biochemist and do medical research. Patricia, Liz's age, will be off to nurse's training this fall. There are five younger children at home. As we talked about their ambitions, Patrick broke in and questioned sadly, "Will none of you want to be farmers?" It was a great visit we had, or, as the Irish would say, a grand visit. Very warm and all too short.

Number six was in the town of Abbeyfeale in County Limerick, where after Sunday mass we fell into step behind the annual Corpus Christi procession and followed it along the highway (holding up traffic for nearly an hour) and around the town square and back to church and into a pub.

In England they measure you a precise shot; in Ireland there are no shot glasses. In England the people are polite; in Ireland the people are friendly. England is a park and London is a wonder. Ireland is a rocky pasture and Dublin is kind of dingy. We rented a car in Ireland and spent seven days on the Irish roads, sharing them with cows, bicyclers, strolling lovers, church processions, ponies pulling carts, sheep, tinkers, and not many cars. Fuel is dear. We stayed at a few bed-and-breakfast houses and thus met the Irish and got more for breakfast than we could hold and saved a hell of a lot of money. If you want to take a bath at a bed-and-breakfast, you give the landlady something like 75¢ and she gives you the plug to the bathtub.

We took a steamship to the Aran Islands and it

rained all day—a soft rain of the right consistency to dilute my glass of Hennessy. It was on the return trip, in the cramped lounge on the lowest deck, that I witnessed the best (and almost the only) ballad singing of our ten days in Ireland. It was a motley collection of young men with two guitars and a repertoire of songs that grew funnier and dirtier as they grew drunker. As we docked in Galway, they were singing one about a blacksmith who shot sparks out of his ass. They were students, I was told, who were returning to the mainland for classes. Later that evening in Galway, I saw two of them helping a drunken third along a wet street under a dim light.

We pursued Yeats here and there and ended up in Sligo, where we arose and went to Innisfree and imagined a small cabin built there and nine bean rows and a hive for the honeybee. It rained and rained. And of course to Drumcliff Churchyard under bare Ben Bulben's head to read the message on Yeats's gravestone: "Cast a cold eye on life, on death, horseman, pass by."

JULY 13   After several hours of horizontal staring today, I have figured some things out about *Jemmy*.

Otis Chapman will have no wife. He will live alone. Jemmy's father will forbid her to sit for a portrait; Mr. Olson will encourage her.

Marty will go back to school (with eight fingers) only after Otis promises a horse. The horse distracts Marty's classmates from his injured hand.

JULY 14   During the weekend I imagined first a short story, then a book-length work based on these letters to Dick Brook and my journal. It was to be called "Journal of a Year Off." Now I'm not sure.

JULY 23   Margaret Lichtenberg, editor at Frederick Warne & Co., says the last chapter of *Pinecone* is still not right. Once more, with feeling.

AUGUST 1976

AUGUST 9   The wind is strong from the east, and the leaves are falling out of the trees. Do botanists understand the death wish of Minnesota leaves? This is the one year out of a score when our leaves might have enjoyed a long life, for it was an early spring and the buds broke open in the middle of April (a month early), and now in early August (a month and a half early) they are falling down dead. On the first day after death, the birch leaf lies luminously yellow on the sunny grass, flat and round like a transparent coin. The second day the leaf is a luminous light brown and curled into a cylinder like the dry husk of a large insect. On the third day the leaf has changed shape once more, having suffered overnight the slow and final convulsions of its stem and veins; it is sharply creased and curled and its color is that of old rust.

Now at the end of (and as justification for) my sabbatical, things are beginning to happen on the writing front. *Travel and Leisure* is paying me $500 for an article describing my visit to Robert Frost's cabin in Vermont. It appears quite certain that *Four Miles to Pinecone*, a novel for young readers I wrote three years ago, will be bought by Frederick Warne, a house specializing in children's books. My prayers, however, concern *Staggerford*, my magnum opus, which at the moment rests on someone's desk at Viking. This is its second stop. I have a rather long letter from Houghton Mifflin in which the first and third paragraphs are devoted to why they almost bought it (perceptive irony, fresh description, marvelous secondary characters) and the longer middle paragraph to why they didn't (too long, the main character uninteresting, loose plot). My agent, God bless her, believes in the book, and should Viking fail us, she has dozens of other places to send it. This is where the agent is a great benefit to mankind; how tiresome and discouraging it would be to have to wrap those 475 pages and send them off every time the mailman returned them to your door. I'd run out of wrapping paper. I'm low on string.

AUGUST 11   I wish I didn't have to go back to teaching. Meeting my classes fourteen hours a week is likely to be distracting. The job of writing is not to be equaled for happiness in the classroom. Nor anywhere else that I can think of.

AUGUST 12   I have the feeling that someone will buy *Staggerford*.

SEPTEMBER 1976

SEPTEMBER 5   On Wednesday I got this telegram:

CONGRATULATIONS. ATHENEUM PUBLISHERS TAK-
ING STAGGERFORD. CALL ME FOR DETAILS. BEST
HARRIET.

My beloved agent. Actually, I didn't get the telegram. My son got it. I was in the middle of cleaning the cabin when he called and read it to me over the phone. I think I was shaking a rug when the phone rang. I was up there with a friend named Chuck, who was washing dishes. (I run a clean cabin.) When I hung up the phone, I shivered and Chuck grinned. It was one o'clock by the clock over my refrigerator, so it was two in New York and Harriet would be returning from lunch. I would give her twenty minutes to get back to her desk. In the meantime, I shook the rest of the rugs and dusted the tables and lamps and the top of the refrigerator and all the windows. Fortunately all the windows are small-paned and dusting them is a lengthy process. One-oh-five. I swept the bathroom floor and the floors in the two bedrooms and the kitchen floor and the porch. I swept the sidewalk. One-ten. I said, "Chuck, I don't know if I believe this." Chuck grinned. Chuck is one of the few people in Minnesota who realizes that speaking to the world via the printed word has been my lifelong dream. Chuck takes a somewhat keener interest in this dream of mine than you would expect from a man who teaches trigonometry. Chuck let the water out of the sink and began wiping the dishes he had washed. One-fifteen. I had forgotten to dust the chairs. I dusted the four chairs around the dining room table, the three chairs in the living room (including the small rocker that tipped over two summers ago and spilled Mr. L., a big neighbor, onto the rug), and the chair in each bedroom. One-nineteen. I called Harriet. As I listened to the sounds of a dozen tiny circuits engaging themselves between Minnesota and Manhattan, it occurred to me that I didn't know how to pronounce Atheneum.

I imagined the switchboard transferring me to Harriet's office. It had to be one of those old upright panels, like pegboard, and out of many of the holes were hanging long black cords, and the operator had to be Miss Mulligan, the fifty-year-old spinster who in the 1940s operated the switchboard in the telephone office next to my father's grocery store. She wound her red-gray hair into a bun at the back of her head and in the bun she wore a comb and we didn't call her an operator. In those days we called her "Central."

She would say, "Number, please," and we would say something like "Central, I'm looking for Dr. Glabe. He isn't at home and he isn't playing bridge over at the Windermeres, so where is he?" And Central would tell you in a dull, uninterested voice, as though after she had learned everything there was to know about everybody in town (which, incidentally, she did know), life held no more interest for her.

Well, it was this same sort of voice three months ago at Harriet's office that had put me in touch with her for the first time. I said that I had been wondering if she had any good news about my fiction, and Harriet replied, her voice measured and far away, "The good news is that I believe in your writing." That was it. Eleven words—if you included "hello"—were all I got. But I ask you, if your agent has set you a quota of eleven words and she has given you your choice of which eleven you would like, wouldn't those be the eleven?

Now it is September. The last circuit locks into place, and after a pause, a sigh, the young girl announces the name of the firm. I ask for Harriet. She sighs again and asks me who I am. She puts me through. Harriet says hello and we both speak at once. I have never been good on the phone and this is going to be one of my more awkward performances. She tells me that Atheneum was the third house to see *Staggerford*. Did she say *Ath*-e-*nee*-um or Ath-*ee*-neum? I can't remember. She said Judith somebody and Robert somebody (or was it Roger? or Reynard?) had read the manuscript, and despite its being too long, they wanted it. I said that was great. She said she had assured them that I would make the necessary cuts. I said that was great. She said they would pay me an advance of $3,000, half of it when I signed the contract and the other half after I made the cuts. I said that was great. Harriet said, "Pardon?" I said that was great. She said Atheneum was a good house, that *Shogun* came from there. I said that was great. Then I said, "Harriet, I'm going to keep you supplied with writing." She said that was great. I told her that next I was going to write a novel about Miss McGee (Pruitt's landlady in *Staggerford*) . She said that was great and she asked me if she could ask me how old I was. I said I was forty-three. She said that was a good age. She was computing, I suppose, how many books I had left in me. I'd love to know the number she came up with. She asked me if I taught at Brainerd Community College and I said yes. "And you were born in Minnesota and you've lived all your life out there?" Yes. "Do you ever come this way?" Oh, yes, I said, I was in New York twenty years ago (actually after I hung up I realized it was thirty-two years ago) and I might go back again someday, one could never tell. For some reason, she was amused. Then we talked for a minute about *Four Miles to Pinecone*, the novel for young adults. She predicted that this was to be the week when we would hear from Frederick Warne. Then I thanked her and we hung up. I shivered again for a second, and Chuck wanted to know the details of our conversation. "Chuck, would you mind if I went for a walk alone?" "Get out of here," he said.

I walked around rather aimlessly in the woods and found myself in a stand of pine trees a mile from the cabin. I half anticipated an emotional reaction to this big news—perhaps some display of tears or crackbrained laughter, the sort of thing that you want to experience by yourself—but there was no hint of such emotion and I returned to the cabin, where Chuck was bent over the oil painting he had begun before lunch. I pulled a chair up to my palette and the 12 × 24-inch canvas on which I had painted a sky and half a prairie and I spent the afternoon lost in that landscape, coming out two or three times for brandy on ice. It turned out to be a rather poor painting.

SEPTEMBER 10   When preparing for my sabbatical, I arranged for fifteen credits with Ken Henriques, professor at Bemidji State; for money (if needed), from Marv Campbell, banker in Brainerd; and I arranged the wording of my sabbatical proposal with the help of Bill Oatey, president of Brainerd Community College. The sabbatical loomed so large before it began; now it is settling into its place with all my other past years. I think of how easy it would have been *not* to have prepared Marie and my parents for my year off, *not* to have written to Ken, *not* to have filled out the Citizens State Bank financial statement, *not* to have consulted Bill Oatey, *not* to have committed myself to driving to New England, *not* to have written *Staggerford*—not to have known the joy of that year.

Marie predicted disaster—lack of money, lack of occupation—but had to admit it wasn't so bad as the year passed.

Mother encouraged me to take the year off; then when she saw how much I enjoyed it, she worried that henceforth I would be discontent with teaching. (Now she is worried that publishing *Staggerford* might change me. Is it typically Irish to worry about good fortune as well as bad?)

The year did not begin well. It started for me at the Roseville Mall, where I displayed paintings for five days.

I recall standing on the upper level of the shopping center, on the mezzanine, you might say, and watching the people passing below me. I stood there for three days, displaying my paintings. The first day I thought watching the people amusing. The second day it struck me that they were all walking in the exact footsteps of the people from the day before, turning their heads at the same displays, visiting the same shops, buying the same products, carrying sacks stamped with the same trademarks. It was like watching bees who in their hive rituals are said to be tracing the same patterns that millions of their ancestors traced. On the second day, I was not amused. I was rather sad to see this illustration of man's predictability. On the third day I was downright grieved. It was a very busy day. Some of the same people were back from the first two days and the noise they made was loud and they produced in the onlooker an impression of vigor and haste and excitement, but it was clear, from the mezzanine, that what they were doing was nothing more than they had done before. True, they were doing it vigorously and hastily and excitedly, but what they were doing was simply tracing the age-old patterns. Where was all this leading them, I asked at my great height. It's leading them to come back tomorrow and do it again, I answered. Well, my point is that that's how I sometimes felt as I was working on *Staggerford*. All my characters were busier than hell, fascinated by what they were doing, preoccupied with one another. But I—I was standing above them watching them go through their paces and seeing that much of what they did wasn't very important. I mean, where did it all get them? At first I was amused. By page 200, I was sad. On page 400 I grieved. Think of God looking down at us from the mezzanine. What strength of character He must possess to preserve Himself from despair.

SEPTEMBER 17   I got word last Saturday that the publisher Frederick Warne will publish *Four Miles to Pinecone*. I have sold, ten days apart, two novels. It's nothing short of a miracle. *Four Miles to Pinecone* is a boy's adventure story. Warne will pay me half of what Atheneum is paying me. I know nothing about the market for children's books, except that libraries make up 80 percent of it. I don't know if there are enough libraries in the world to earn me over $1,500. But to be read is what I've been striving for. How many times have I said to myself: It is neither fame nor fortune that I seek in linking words together on paper, it is to be read. It is to extend my voice out beyond the range of my voice. It is to have six people in Missouri and four in Idaho see, for a little while, the world the way I see it. For years I have been practicing to be good enough to deserve their attention, and now I will come to the attention of those six people in Missouri and those four in Idaho, and I have my reward. The money is nice. It may buy me time off from teaching. But it is nothing compared to the thought of being read.

OCTOBER 1976

OCTOBER 7   A month ago I stepped back onto the campus and merged back into the faculty and into the classroom as though I had never been gone. How does it feel to be back? they asked me then and they ask me now. Fine, I said then. Fine, I say now. But it isn't all that fine. I say fine because I know that one way to become (or to become *more*) discontented is to *act* discontented, to say horseshit instead of fine. I will not be tempted down that trail. That way lies first discontent, then despair. I will continue to say Fine, and when I'm in the classroom, I'll give it all I've got.

But I, like Lazarus, have come back from the other side. I have known what it is like to have months—whole uninterrupted months—at this little old Smith-Corona, and when it comes to things that are really downright fine, well . . . So what I'm trying to do is to be a worthy teacher when I'm in the classroom (fifteen hours per week) and to put teaching out of my mind for the rest of the hours of the week. If I'm going to do everything I did last year and teach besides, then I cannot afford any more than fifteen hours' distraction. Perhaps I will find that it's impossible to accomplish all I did last year.

I am typing the fourth draft of *Staggerford* at the rate of twenty pages a day. I got it back from Atheneum with twenty-four suggestions (large suggestions, small suggestions) for revision, and I am preparing them the final draft. I agree with virtually all the suggestions. Somebody at Atheneum must have studied *Staggerford* day and night. "How can you say this on page 403 when you have said that on page 87?" I think Atheneum knows *Staggerford* better than I do. I am on page 180, a bit over one-third of the way.

O*CTOBER 8* It is one of those months with no spare minutes, no spare seconds, fielding letters and phone calls from New York . . . teaching creative writing, poetry, grammar, intro to literature . . . exhibiting paintings twice (Little Falls and St. Paul) . . . keeping the lid on the household ... walking to and from work (four miles a day, my only chance for solitude) ... typing yet another draft of *Staggerford* ... visiting my parents once or twice a week.

I don't believe I or my habits or attitudes have changed since the *Staggerford/Pinecone* news, but certain people around me seem to have been affected—as though a bomb had been dropped with the point of the explosion not affected as much as the perimeter of the blast.

Joe Plut dwells on my publishing success every day in every class.

Mother worries about my overworking, worries about interrupting my work, and (finally today) worries about worrying about interrupting my work.

OCTOBER 10   There must be other "types" like Superintendent of Staggerford High School Ansel Stevenson that I could develop in my fiction. The novels of Evelyn Waugh are full of them:

The slovenly officer whose clothes fit worse as the day went on. The rough and ready one-eyed officer whose appetite for combat was not courageous but pathological. The cowardly officer who hid in a culvert.

Ansel Stevenson came out of Conrad's *The Shadow Line,* the first mate with the bad heart.

My teaching colleagues provide inspiration for characters:

1. The compulsive, useless motions of Mac.
2. The argumentative spirit of Mark—the color rising up the back of his neck.
3. The bringing in of past experience of Jerry. "This is the way we did it in Kiester."
4. Saying everything twice, like Joe and Dennis.

5. The exaggerated formality of Dr. Cheng, shaking hands every morning and night with his colleagues.
6. Al watching the football films—clickety, sputter, buzz, goes the projector. His constant refrain of "I wish I could sit here all day."

OCTOBER 11   Sitting on the cabin porch, in the sun, having shaken hands with former student Steve Gravdahl, having dismantled the mailbox, having raked a small square of leaves, sitting now in the swing, in the mottled shade of the pine tree, having typed ten more pages of the *Staggerford* revision, having brought—in my mind—*Staggerford*'s tooth-pulling episode to a "different" conclusion (Imogene talked all the way home about the size of women, the styles for winter, the origins of dentistry, and the harnessing of atomic energy, changing the subject at fifty-mile intervals; Miles, at fifty-mile intervals, ate aspirin), having last night eaten lasagna and cake in a neighbor's house trailer, having contracted heartburn, having gone to sleep reading Belloc's *Path to Rome* (leaving him standing on his fourth or fifth hill), having awakened at three-twenty and read more Belloc (following him to summits of four or five more hills), then falling asleep at four-twenty.

I'm sipping hot coffee in the swing now, having just noticed on the porch floor the fly that yesterday was walking in circles but which now has turned over on his back and died.

OCTOBER 12   And now I am on page 230, halfway through the *Staggerford* revision.

For the second weekend in a row I have packed my typewriter in my car with a pound of bacon and a pound of cheese and come up here to the cabin. Alone. In days gone by I was always trailing kids behind me. And even today, I guess I would be trailing David behind me, for this is the season for shooting ducks and partridge, and there are ducks and partridge around the cabin; but there is no hunting this year. The Department of Natural Resources opened the season for five days (long enough for all of us to buy our hunting licenses) and then they closed it. In the northern half of Minnesota there are currently 216 fires burning.

I am going out to walk two and a half miles to a high hill in the middle of a hayfield and lie down in the weeds under the sun and try to figure out what I am going to write when I finish revising *Staggerford*. Later, when I get back here to the cabin I will knock back a large slug of brandy, put two pork chops in the frying pan, and then make myself a lettuce and radish salad. And toast. This kind of day is the next thing to heavenly bliss. I should have been a hermit.

OCTOBER 21   Yesterday, or what I think of as the anniversary of the beginning of *Staggerford*, I finished typing the fourth draft; then late in the afternoon after most of the staff went home from the college, I duplicated nearly 200 pages on a malfunctioning machine. Then I sat in my office through the supper hour, proofreading, until Mike came to me for help: he had run out of gas—a problem it took me two and a half hours to solve with my customary inefficiency. Suffice it to say that this morning two of my cars and two of my shoes reeked of gasoline.

NOVEMBER 1976

NOVEMBER 1, ALL SAINTS' DAY The other day I was displaying my paintings in the gymnasium of the Park Rapids Middle School along with a hundred other exhibitors and exhibitionists at what is known as the Annual Park Rapids North Star Arts and Crafts Show, the crafts outnumbering the arts ten to one, when I decided to walk down the old familiar hall and have a look at my old familiar classroom, 102. I was standing there gazing into that room when Bob Heeren of all people came up behind me and said, "What are you doing, reliving your past?" and I told him yes, that's what I was doing, and he assumed, I'm sure, that I was reliving the events of the early sixties, and I didn't bother to tell him that the events I was reliving were the events of last winter that took place on my typing table in my den in Brainerd, fictional events with room 102 at the center of them. I found it strangely moving to be standing there looking at the setting of a good deal of what happens in the book. I mean my time in Park Rapids is much farther back in the past than my writing of that novel; I was recalling fictional events such as Jeff Norquist's jumping out the window and Beverly Bingham's book report on *Gone with the Wind* and Miles Pruitt's standing on hall duty. With the passing of time, reality will once again supersede fiction, I'm sure, but it was fun to step for a minute into my novel.

Last night in church as I watched the parish file up the middle aisles to communion, I looked for the real-life counterpart of Miss McGee, for she is devout and certainly would have been there. I saw a number of wrinkles and white hair, but they were too stooped or too jowly or too slow-footed or, in most cases, too heavy to be Miss McGee. Miss McGee is skinny and quick. I saw one woman with the beak and the light-boned quickness of a bird, but she was barely five feet tall, and I think Miss McGee is taller than that. I expect, though, that I will eventually see her. The parish is large.

NOVEMBER 3 Unlike most occasions in the past when I felt it was time to begin writing something but I couldn't think of anything to write about, I am now having trouble choosing among several possibilities.

Shall I write a lengthy article entitled "The Record of a Year Off," pasted together from journal entries? Shall I write a lengthy travel article about Ireland? (I have been working on one for a month, but it keeps stopping in the middle of the road.) Shall I write the definitive novel on the befuddling changes in the Catholic Church with Miss McGee, my favorite fictional spinster, at the center of them? Shall I go back to the adolescent novel, *Jemmy*, I began last spring but which petered out in the summer on page 50? The one thing I am not tempted to embark upon is, strange to say, a short story. *Staggerford* seems to have caused channels to shift in my brain. That novel has caused me to think primarily in terms of book-length work. For six years I wrote nothing but short stories, envisioned nothing but short stories in the future, but *Staggerford* changed that. It was like dragging a stick through the mud in April and shifting the course of the stream of melting snow. Of course embarking on any writing project at the present time is scary as hell after what's happened to *Staggerford*. Can I do it again? I ask myself day and night. I'm half scared to try, so my concern about what to start writing is probably only a delaying tactic, an attempt to put off the moment of truth.

The other day in my creative writing class, after one of the students performed three of his compositions for us, accompanying himself on the guitar, I launched into a sermon about sustained effort—working hard and steadily in order to get good at something. "Ted's ability to play the guitar," I said (his playing had really knocked us out), "it didn't just happen; he worked hard to get that good." The class nodded. "And writing," I said, "if writing is a talent it is only ten percent talent; it is ninety percent training, work, energy, effort, desire, and determination." The class nodded. "And teaching," I said . . . but I could say no more. I had just destroyed my argument by bringing up teaching. Isn't it the damnedest thing how successful teaching has almost nothing to do with training and experience in the classroom? Assuming one has mastered the subject matter, which is necessary in all professions, there is absolutely no assurance that one will teach well, whether it's the first class of one's career or the last class of one's fortieth year.

NOVEMBER 10   Letter to Gordon Lish, fiction editor of *Esquire*:

> I have just sold two novels. Atheneum will publish *Staggerford*, in which the reader is taken further down Main Street and higher Up the Down Staircase; and Frederick Warne will publish *Four Miles to Pinecone*, a tale for young readers.
>   This is to acknowledge the part you played in my good fortune. After you picked me out of *Prairie Schooner* magazine nearly four years ago, I sent you several stories which were *almost*

good enough, culminating in "The Cheerleader," which *almost* made it into the big sports issue of '74. (Remember the boy who while trying to seduce the cheerleader in her father's woodworking shop, got his new suit chewed to shreds in the bandsaw?) It's now part of *Staggerford*. How fortuitous that instead of returning "The Cheerleader" to me you gave it to Harriet Wasserman, who now represents me in the marketplace.

How absolutely essential to my career that you were reading my stuff in those days.

How tragic for fiction that *Esquire* has closed its gates to beginners.

NOVEMBER 18 Yesterday—a rare good day for writing. I rewrote pages 40 through 49 of *Jemmy*. The Chapmans, after nearly a year's stalemate, have come alive. Kathy Chapman is skittish; Otis is large and good-natured. (I see now that Kathy is not the right name for her. Kathys to me are prettier and younger than Mrs. Chapman.)

NOVEMBER 20 It is that week between the last cold spell of fall and the first cold spell of winter. The trees are bare of leaves and birds, and strips of old socks are stuffed around the loose storm windows. Flags hang limp and frost turns to water under the climbing sun. It is that week when it seems that summer, which we assumed was dead, is gathering its strength to reappear. It is like that time in the decline of a cancer victim when he loses his pain and his color comes back. Although you know better than to hope, you can't help hoping.

It is that week when the end of fall quarter looms

ahead, when the student papers you have been stuffing into your desk must be brought out for examination, when potential questions for the final exams begin to take shape in your head, when you avoid looking back on your writing accomplishments because you know what you'll find: 80 percent of your energies poured into teaching, 20 percent into writing—and you had been determined to do things the other way around.

It is that week before your father's eightieth birthday, and you wonder what you can give him that's out of the ordinary. So little must seem out of the ordinary when you are eighty.

NOVEMBER 21 I am busy to the point of distraction. My problem is that I am trying to do everything I did last year and teach besides. I mean I can't see setting aside painting and writing for the sake of teaching, for although teaching is where the money is, painting and writing are where the fun is. So I am pulled in three directions and feeling a bit desperate about it all. For example, I'm forty-nine pages into another novel, but I'll have to let it hang fire in order to turn out fifteen to twenty paintings for the show at the Touche Gallery in Bemidji, which begins December 5. And meanwhile make my way through stacks of student compositions.

NOVEMBER 26 It's the end of one of those days when I planned to do a lot and didn't do a damned thing. Up at 6:30. Read two short stories in the December *Esquire*, neither of which I can understand. Ate a bowl of breakfast food, one slice of toast, a cup of coffee. Sketched a lighthouse in preparation for painting a 20 × 30 oil for an old lady in St. Paul whose best friend once leased the island on which the lighthouse stands, an Apostle Island. Now the friend is dead and the old lady wants a painting of the place and gives me three photos to go by. My horizon tilts to the left; the lighthouse leans to the right. It's one of those days.

I contemplate all that I haven't done today. For one thing, I had intended to get at least to page 68 of *Jemmy*. I read the first page of an article by a man who lives part of every year in a village in Spain. It's a good article, so I quit reading. You see, it's turning into one of those days when I must punish myself for not having done anything. Do you ever have those days, Dick? It sounds very stupid and it's probably bad for one's mental health, but with my free time so goddamn precious this year, I can't seem to allow myself a day off. I cannot allow myself to read the article about the man in the Spanish village because I haven't *earned* it. Had I painted a picture or written three pages, I could now read the article with an easy conscience. Outside my window, dusk becomes darkness. I can't easily allow dusk to become darkness either, but days end whether I permit them to or not. I have not the power to hold back night, and I resent that.

Last year was different. Last year I had fifteen consecutive months of free time. Not one day was all that precious. Never once did I resent the coming of night; in fact, I often went walking at dusk through the snow to relish the dying cold light in the west.

Which is better: to drive oneself to one's limits, writing and teaching and painting until one tires and feels guilt for being tired; or to give up writing?

NOVEMBER 27   I'm up to page 72 of *Jemmy*, now entitled "The Maiden of Eagle Brook." Jemmy is home from the Chapmans' and the little ones are home from the Roosters'. What next? Stott must paint the Chapmans' barn. Maybe Candy can entice him to do it.

DECEMBER 1976

DECEMBER 3   This business of publishing a book is more rewarding than anything in my life. It has to do with the length of time from acceptance to publication— the series of pleasures building to the book itself. Seeing the jacket for *Pinecone*, I felt a slight emotion. The full impact I expect when I hold *Staggerford* in my hands— "great pleasure in an instant and deepening pleasure thereafter," I read somewhere.

DECEMBER 12   On the community college level, my having written a novel makes me suspect. There are two people where I work who understand the accomplishment of writing a novel. The rest are not at all pleased. My writing, to them, is like pneumonia; either I will recover and settle back into my prescribed mold, or the malady will worsen and adversely affect my teaching. In years past, I taught two freshman classes and two sophomore classes each quarter; coming back from my year off I find myself with three freshman and one sophomore. In years past I used to have a late schedule, so that I could write or paint until ten A.M. This year my classes are scattered through the day from dawn to dusk.

I have been asked to come to Bemidji State for a day and be their annual English Week speaker; to do this I will have to sacrifice a day's pay at Brainerd. It isn't a writer's environment. But it's the environment I have chosen and I will see it through. After all, I was on the staff of a four-year college and found I could not survive without a Ph.D. Concerning Brainerd, I am dealing with the above complaints in this manner: (a) I continue to teach what I always taught, whether the course is called a freshman course or a sophomore course. For example, I used to have a sophomore course in which I taught, among other things, *Othello*. Now with that course snatched away from me, I simply teach *Othello* to the freshmen. (b) I am learning to write at school, in my office, on a typewriter I filched. Because my classes go from early to late, there are necessarily large gaps between some of them, during which gaps I shut my door and invent fiction. (c) I will not mind giving up a day's pay to return to Bemidji State College where I used to teach—the fun of it, the irony of it, a former instructor and English Club advisor coming back as the English Week speaker.

DECEMBER 31   While you work on the first draft you don't have a clear idea of the work as whole. You're pushing yourself down a foggy road and you are risking losing it all with a false step, but you can't be responsible for what lies ahead in the fog. In the second draft you are responsible for every inch of road from beginning to end, because the fog has lifted and with each step you must look ahead to the limits of your vision. Can Miles Pruitt say this on page 148 and still die with dignity on page 402?

JANUARY 1977

JANUARY 15   John Dos Passos in a letter: "You start out with a few notions and anecdotes about somebody you know and then other scraps of the lives of other people get in and a large slice of your own life and then if you are lucky the mash begins to ferment and becomes something quite different."

In their letters, American writers continually speak of wishing they could see each other. It has to do with the size of the country. British writers are always within an hour's train ride of each other.

The long political segments of Dos Passos's letters interest me not at all. My eye goes directly to his account of human relationships, landscapes, and reflections on writing.

FEBRUARY 1977

FEBRUARY 15 A letter from Harriet yesterday. "Thanks for the travel piece," she said, "it's fun.

"Send me *Jemmy*," she said.

Staggerford is in the hands of her agent for movies and her British agent.

FEBRUARY 28 In plumbing the sea of my imagination (forgive the extravagant metaphor) I discovered an undertow of melancholy. Not unlike what I felt during my five days in the Roseville Mall. It must derive from standing back from, or above, life—watching the movements of human endeavor. How does God do it? How does He ward off melancholy? Is that why He hides His face from us—to conceal His sorrow? Perhaps the Old Testament prophets who seemed to know God better than we do were correct in portraying Him as temperamental.

The amazing capacity of Joe's mind and stomach. Yesterday in Minneapolis we stuffed ourselves with drama (*The National Health* and *The Winter's Tale*) and food (Jax and The Normandy).

MARCH 1977

MARCH 1 *Staggerford* has been chosen as a Book-of-the-Month Club alternate. It must be a good book.

MARCH 10 Blue Cloud Abbey, South Dakota: Brain operated yesterday at half speed. Revised two and a half chapters of *Jemmy*—a superficial revision, two brand-new sentences on page 1 exhausting my creativity. Drank less brandy with my friend, Brother Benet, last night, so today I will do better.

Today two young artists, Brother Micah and Brother Sebastian, showed me their weaving. Sebastian introduced me to Sister Somebody, his cousin, saying, "Jon is a writer." My reaction was embarrassment. I'll have to get over that.

Said Father Francis, the questmaster, this morning, as I passed through the lounge reading a manuscript page, "Are you finding enough peace and quiet?"

"Plenty. It's great," I said.

This is what the abbey has, besides prayer, to offer—peace and quiet. Who where I come from understands its value? Who here does? On the outside, peace and quiet doesn't exist. Here it is so plentiful as to be held cheap. Only outsiders coming in can take its measure, weigh its worth.

MARCH 27 My colleague Hazelle hugged me in the hallway as my son Mike handed me the first finished copy of *Pinecone*.

News of the State Arts Award: $750 for the first twenty-five pages of *Jemmy*. Bodes well for the finished book, I think. News last Monday of *McCall's* printing a part of *Staggerford*: $1,500. Wow, my seven years of hard labor are paying off.

MARCH 28   Good novels, like good poems, good short stories, are irreducible.

APRIL 1977

APRIL 12   Most recent sign of spring's return: snow-bank's disappearance from yard, March 29. Interesting developments:

Check from *McCall's* for $1,350.

London publisher offers £1,000 for *Staggerford*.

Galleys from *McCall's*.

Invitation from *Library Journal* to contribute to first-novelist article.

Eleven copies of *Four Miles to Pinecone* arrive on my birthday. The campus bookstore orders twenty-four, sells out in one day.

I mail *Jemmy* to Harriet on Easter Monday.

Received two messages on Friday—a letter of praise from my London publisher, Piers Burnett, in which he writes: "A novel so beautifully written, so accomplished, so straightforward." And a note of reprimand from the dean. "We missed you at our breakfast meeting," he says. "We're meeting again Tuesday. Be there with materials." Be where? What materials?

MAY 1977

MAY 3   My friend and colleague Forrest Robinson is dying. His suit coat hangs on his spine as though on a hook. I spoke to his class and said, among other things,

"I killed off Miles Pruitt because I didn't know what else to do with him." In the first place, I'm not sure it's true, and in the second place, it must have been a horrible thing for a dying man to hear—my making light of life, of death. The class laughed, as I had hoped. Forrest, bless him, didn't bat an eye.

MAY 14 A year ago I wouldn't have believed this week's mail possible:

Harriet's critique of *Jemmy*, the André Deutsch contract, the *New York Times* and *Publishers Weekly* reviews of *Staggerford*, and the $750 creative writing award from the Minnesota State Arts Board.

And the week before that: the *Staggerford* jacket, the "Dingle" galleys from *The New York Times*, and the *McCall's* illustration for Miss McGee.

Incredible good fortune and, of course, answered prayers.

JUNE 1977

JUNE 1 I have passed a week or more of feeling lazy. Not tired exactly, but not compulsive about writing. Probably it's a rest after *Staggerford* and *Jemmy*.

JULY 1977

JULY 7 Four days of forced enslavement at my typewriter, an attempt to prove Joan Didion's theory that four days will produce the beginning of a worthy piece of fiction. An attempt to have something fictional in hand, no matter how tiny, before I begin my two-week stint at Bemidji Writers' Workshop.

JULY 25   *Staggerford*'s publication day.

Up at seven-thirty, the morning refreshingly cool, the sun bright, the wind north. Watered petunias, then walked to church. Father Hollenhorst, in the third week of his priesthood, has finally learned how to put on his vestments. The old man with the shakes came in late, knocking his cane against the pews and stopping every few feet to correct his line of progress, for he has a tendency to drift to his left.

JULY 31   To Powers Department Store in Minneapolis with daughter Liz, Dayton's Department Store in Burnsville for book signings. I've decided my fourth book will be about heroic acts in old age. Some work of noble note before the end. *Ulysses*.

AUGUST 1977

AUGUST 9   On the way home tonight I stopped at the library and read the latest *New York Times Book Review*. I skimmed, uninterested in all but a tribute to Borges and an account of Stephen King's success with occult novels. How long will I continue to dote on *Staggerford* at the expense of other novels I wish to write?

AUGUST 25   I have tried to begin Novel Four, floundering. I have had two writing days so far this week. I need a hundred. Jim McNutt, my friend the architect, tells me his favorite line from *Staggerford*: "To befriend an Indian, feed him pie."

SEPTEMBER 1977

SEPTEMBER 18   One of my first public functions as an author is at the Radisson fashion show in Minneapolis, of all things. The parade of thin women down the runway was interrupted now and then by interviews with local celebrities such as Miss USA, a cartoonist, and me. I had been told to arrive backstage at 9:45 A.M., so at the appointed time I led my son Mike, along for the ride, through what looked like a backstage door and we found ourselves in a dingy room full of milling models, some of them naked. We retreated and were shown to chairs by a tall woman in a brown suit. We were introduced to the cartoonist Dick Guindon and Eleanor Brenner, who dresses the vice president's wife.

The show began, newspaper columnist Barbara Flanagan at the mike, models of all ages, colors, and sexes strutting overhead on the runway. There were music and applause when I was introduced and I burst onstage in my old rags: blue blazer from Kmart, blue shirt from JCPenney. Barbara Flanagan and I sat at a table during the interview, and though my voice didn't shake, the water in Barbara's glass did whenever I put my elbows on the table. We raffled off five books and I exited to applause and music.

Miss USA said to me, "I want you to know that every morning you make me laugh." This was spoken very seriously, like a queen. It flashed through my mind that she read a page of *Staggerford* each day, then I saw her mistake. "I'm not the cartoonist," I said. "I'm the novelist." She backed away, flustered. Perhaps her first flustered moment since her coronation. The look on her face was that of someone who had fallen into a ditch. I walked away leaving Mike to pull her out. He has always loved beauty queens. "I remember the night you won," he said to her gallantly.

JANUARY 1978

JANUARY 22   Winter quarter has not yet worn me down, for I still feel at the top of my writing powers. Novel Four will remain interrupted so that I may write another draft of *Jemmy* for Margaret McElderry, my editor for young adult books.

JANUARY 30   Having written four pages of *Jemmy* between seven and nine this morning, I found it easier to go off to my first class than it was last week, when I felt very low on Monday morning.

Having grown up in a houseful of people, one wants company all his life. Having grown up alone, I treasure solitude. With others I am often bored, alone never.

My urge to read and write has become so powerful that all my other interests (athletics, painting, photography, fishing) seem to have dimmed. Unless I am with someone who shares my passion for reading and writing, I can scarcely disguise my lack of interest in our conversation. Except to two or three people, I have become worthless as a comrade, but I hope I have become good company to my readers.

What have my twenty-two years of dedicated teaching meant to the world? Nothing, I sometimes think. Has teaching been only a device to keep my mind diverted and my family fed? A profession for my own benefit and no one else's? Or have I changed the attitudes of nearly a generation of young people—given them an awareness of themselves through literature?

Whenever I weigh the effect of my own teachers, no one of them seems to have made any considerable contribution (except in the first three grades), although their cumulative efforts proved to be of great consequence. I can think of no other profession where the rewards are so intangible.

Reading my readers. My audience is almost entirely women—where have we failed in educating men in the humanities?

Years ago I was interested in the idea of rhyme. Why, especially as children, do we find rhyme so delightful? But now after bringing the subject up twice a year in poetry class, I can hardly stand to think of it.

Is this because ideas grow threadbare from being talked about too much? Or is the damage caused by sharing your ideas with "unformed minds" (Edmund Wilson's term for students)? I suspect it's the former. For each of us, ideas, like clothes, wear out.

Writing and teaching. After a weekend of writing I can get at least a little morning writing done before class on Monday and Tuesday, but by Wednesday my imagination has begun to revolt against the stop-start pattern and I can do nothing more until the next Saturday. Oh, to have another six months off next year. But I'm flat broke. And Liz will need piles of tuition money for college.

Perhaps I shall buy time next year and ask for a quarter off. Become a part-time teacher? Or shall I teach a full year and put an end to my money worries?

MARCH 1978

MARCH 15 The Ides. Blue Cloud Abbey. Sausage and sauerkraut last night. Pancakes this morning.

Worked on *Jemmy* from eight until two. Another two days like this and I could finish it. I have forty pages to go, and they will require more cutting than creating. Then the last chapter. Jemmy's thoughts have to be just right—wise but not overwise.

APRIL 1978

APRIL 17 To Chicago last Tuesday to accept the $1,000 Friends of America Writers Award. FAW are 175 bejeweled and gracious women who know a good cause when they see one. With my writing profits I buy time for more writing, and their money will buy me a month next winter. (February, to be exact. December and January have been bought and paid for by Atheneum and *McCall's*.) Along with the money they gave me a lettuce salad, two blueberry tarts, two strips of bacon, and a slice of delicious green pie. In return, they got a twenty-minute account of how *Staggerford* came to be written. A totally enjoyable experience. I took my daughter Liz along. The president of FAW and her husband put us up overnight in their swank condominium—nine floors above Lake Michigan and three floors below Saul Bellow. Fine weather, smooth flying.

JUNE 1978

JUNE 15 Mark Serani, our local bookseller, is trying to interest the Fawcett salesman in *Staggerford*. I have provided him with copies of reviews and articles and the Chicago award. As I went through my files on *Staggerford*, I became more puzzled than ever why a paperback company has not expressed interest. It must be that Atheneum didn't try very hard.

To Nevis from the cabin yesterday by bike, a distance of five miles. I took my place in church between an old lady and a small girl, and eight wood ticks crawled out of my sleeves and out of the collar of my shirt. They came one at a time so I could tear their heads off individually, and I think I did so with no one noticing. Two more ticks after I got home and two more this morning—a total of twelve from my half-mile walk through the brush between the road and the bike trail.

JUNE 21 Yesterday *Staggerford* was published in London.

A sensation of deep pleasure this morning. While I was lying late in bed, the mailman came early—8:45—and rang the doorbell. David answered and paid him 77¢ postage due, and then came to the bedroom and spilled mail across the covers: two letters from Harriet, one having cost a total $2.11 for special delivery, and the other having cost 15¢—both mailed the same day. The special delivery letter said Atheneum is paying me a $3,000 advance for *Jemmy.* Harriet's other letter said *McCall's* would like an Agatha McGee story for Christmas.

Such fun turning on my lamp and propping myself up on my pillow and picking these joyous messages from the folds of the bedspread. Liz and David exclaiming about *Jemmy* as they dart in and out of the bedroom like a couple of swallows.

Afterword

~⌒

I assume that *Staggerford*'s life as a published hard-back was shortened somewhat by its unfavorable re-view in *The New York Times*. Although the *Times* has looked kindly on most of my work, my first novel (as well as my most recent, *The Dean's List*) did not meet with their reviewer's approval. While admitting that "there is something likable about the novel itself," Joyce Carol Oates found my characters "rather close to being two-dimensional, and there are times when nothing at all seems to be happening on the page." The novel "begins strongly but soon wanes, fragmenting into a series of unexceptional scenes reminiscent of television."

Staggerford was received almost everywhere else with enthusiasm. Eugenia Thornton, in the Cleveland *Plain Dealer*, called it "an absolutely smashing first novel . . . an altogether successful work, witty, intelli-gent, compassionate."

Atheneum printed 7,500 copies, and within a month they had disappeared from bookstores. A year later, I found fifteen copies of *Staggerford* on a remainder table at B. Dalton. The price being $1.95, a much better deal than I was getting from my publisher, I carried all fif-teen to the checkout counter, where the clerk said sar-donically, "You must really like this book."

"Oh, I do," I said, "I wrote it." I opened the back flap and showed her my photo.

Whereupon she summoned the manager from the back room—to meet me, I assumed. But no. She said to him, "Would you okay the check this man is writing?"

Staggerford remained out of print for nearly a decade until Ballantine Books brought out the first paperback edition in 1986. Since then, it has gone back to press fifteen times.

As my finances permitted, after the publication of *Staggerford*, I began teaching a reduced load of classes in order to feed my addiction to writing. And that was more or less the pattern of my life for the next twenty years, until my retirement from the classroom in 1997—for I had discovered my reason for writing. It is to write. By this, I mean that my writing income granted me the pleasure—indeed, the privilege—of doing every day what I was born to do, namely to sit here at my desk, picking through the language and finding the best way of expressing what's on my mind, in my memory, in my imagination.

ABOUT THE AUTHOR

JON HASSLER is Regent's Professor Emeritus at St. John's University, Minnesota, and lives with his wife, Gretchen, in Minneapolis. He is also the author of nine widely acclaimed novels: *Staggerford*, *Simon's Night*, *The Love Hunter*, *A Green Journey*, *Grand Opening*, *North of Hope*, *Dear James*, *Rookery Blues*, and *The Dean's List*.